VOICE OF GOD

40-Day Hearing God
ACTIVATION MANUAL

A 40-Day Journey of Practical
Activation in Interacting with God

Art Thomas
James Loruss
Jonathan Ammon

SUPERNATURAL TRUTH PRODUCTIONS, LLC
Practical Training for Spirit-Filled Living
www.SupernaturalTruth.com

Acknowledgements:

Art Thomas:

I'd like to say a huge thanks to my wife, Robin, who pushed me to finish this book (and the movie) during the times when I felt like doing other, less-important things. Her unwavering support and listening ear were vital to the development of this book's content. I also want to thank my parents—Gaylord and Linda Thomas—for demonstrating what it is to listen to the voice of the Lord and Pastor Dan Vander Velde for doing more to train me in prophetic ministry than anyone else besides Jesus.

James Loruss:

I'd like to thank my wife, Connie, for encouraging me and challenging me to hear God's voice in the scriptures more than anyone I've ever met—the Lord knew what I needed; my parents for leading their family well with childlike obedience to the Father; my pastor, Brooks McElhenny, for modeling a daily pursuit to know more of God; my best friend, Jesus, for considering me someone worth speaking to.

Jonathan Ammon:

Thanks to Jesus for loving me, correcting me, and redeeming all the times I've gotten it wrong. Thank you to my wife, Tatiana, for her unwavering support and reminding me that hearing God isn't complicated. Thanks to my parents, Clay and Becky Ammon, for imparting an unshakable belief that God will answer when we call.

Table of Contents

Introduction

When we produced our first movie, *Paid in Full*, we had no idea that God would use it in the ways He did. Through the film itself, we've received reports of people being healed of a variety of ailments, including incurable diseases like cancer and deafness. We've received testimonies of entire churches being activated in healing ministry after watching the film. Through people sharing the movie, churches providing public viewings, and multiple airings on international television, tens of thousands of people have been trained to minister healing in Jesus' name! It has been a humbling journey to say the least!

Of an equal thrill to us were the countless testimonies that came from people walking through the 40-Day Healing Ministry Activation Manual. Many described meaningful encounters with God during the prayer times and journal entries. Thousands started regularly practicing healing ministry.

One man wrote to us with a simply unbelievable testimony. In one of the daily activities in the book, we challenged the reader to use some sort of social media to minister healing to someone. This man decided to reach a bit farther and created a Facebook "Page" about the healing power of Jesus and market it in a region of the world that is almost all Muslim. Hundreds of thousands have "liked" the page because of the message of healing, and many have received healing and engaged in deep discussions about the Son of God.

All this happened within the first year of *Paid in Full* being released.

When we saw the mind-blowing results of our first movie and "Activation Manual," we knew that we needed to create more media to train and equip the Body of Christ to live effectively like Jesus.

In your hands is the first installment of that realization. Along with our movie, *Voice of God*, we have written this book to be more than a mere study of a topic. There are already plenty of teachings "about" hearing God's voice. Our desire was to produce something practical that would actually lead people into encounters with the Lord.

Every day in this book will be an invitation into a deeper relationship with the God who created you. *You were born for this.* As you walk through the lessons and pray through the "prayer starters" — and as you write your journal entries and engage in the daily challenges — you're sure to recognize the nearness of the Lord as He transforms you, your family, and your world.

We've attempted to write each lesson in a way that new and seasoned believers alike can benefit and experience God. This book is not so much a collection of teachings as it is a daily launch pad into encounters with the God who loves you.

Do I Need to Watch the Movie
Voice of God to Benefit from this Book?

We purposely designed this book to stand alone as a powerful tool to help people learn to hear, discern, and respond to God's voice. If you've never seen our movie, *Voice of God,* that's perfectly alright! This book will still offer you a complete training in interacting with God.

With that said, the two-part documentary we made has been an eye-opener for many people, and no book can accomplish what happens when you actually witness miracles happening — not to mention, we're only three people sharing our experiences while the movie presents insights from about fifty. If there is a reasonable way for you to see our film about hearing and knowing God, we highly recommend it. The full movie can be ordered at www.SupernaturalTruth.com.

Ways to Use this Book

This book is not the Bible (nor would we ever claim that it is!). That means you don't have to feel like you must accomplish every prescribed activity. The exercises in this book are merely practical helps for interacting with God that we hope and believe will be beneficial to you if you choose to do them. Each lesson is written to spur you on toward love and good deeds. (See Hebrews 10:24.)

This book is a tool in your hands that you can feel free to use any way you like, but the information is presented in a recommended, systematic, and progressive format based on what we believe will be the most effective path to learning and healthy experiences.

Given that, there are two recommended ways for using this book:

First, you may choose to go through this training as a matter of personal devotional study and enrichment. In this case, the best way to read it is to first watch the film and then read one lesson per day for the next 40 days. There's nothing wrong with starting the study before watching the film, but seeing the movie is perhaps the best way to get your feet wet regarding this topic. If you miss a day or two, simply pick back up where you left off. There's no requirement to actually finish in only 40 days!

Second, while this book stands alone as its own text, it is also designed to serve as supplemental reading that accompanies our 10-week *Voice of God* DVD Small Group Study, which can be purchased at www.SupernaturalTruth.com. In order to make the lessons in this book line up with the small group curriculum, begin reading "Day 1" after the second small group meeting (where you will watch Episode 2 of *Voice of God* together); and then only read one section (five lessons) per week. The lessons you study that week will help fuel discussion at your next meeting because you will have been thinking about and acting on that topic for several days already.

We recommend reading in the morning because of the "Action Step" at the end of each lesson, which should be accomplished somehow that day. If you prefer to read at night, be sure to look again at the "Action Step" the next morning so that it's fresh in your mind throughout the day. The Action Steps are perhaps the most important parts because we generally learn much more through experience than through mere reading. Be sure to journal about your experiences for the sake of personal memory and declaring the wonders of God.

If you ever find yourself missing an Action Step, you can do one of two things: (1) Wait to read the next lesson until you fulfill the challenge presented in the Action Step, or (2) Somehow mark that page of the book and return to it later.

In short, there are a couple ways we designed this book to be used, but ultimately it is a tool in your hands that you can feel free to use however is most beneficial to you.

Are You Ready?

Voice of God is more than a couple episodes of interviews; it's an experience. The same is true of this book. In your hands is an invitation to a deeper relationship with the Father, Son, and Holy Spirit. More than that, it is a vehicle into encounters with the Lord through which He can turn you into a world-changing partner in His work of supernaturally loving the world.

The three of us are in this journey right alongside you. We've each invested years of our lives into learning to hear and discern God's voice. Our goal in this 40-day journey is to hand off to you some of the most important lessons we've learned along the way. We're not coming as "experts" who are somehow better than you; we're coming as fellow travelers who want to better your journey by sharing the mountaintops and valleys that we've already witnessed along the road. We're believing that the Lord will take you much farther than any of us have experienced, and we're honored to have been welcomed to join you for this stretch of the road.

Our prayer for you is that this book will be a catalyst for many encounters with the Lord, both in your quiet times alone with Him and out in public as you act on your relationship with Him. We're expecting miracles, prophetic words, dreams, visions, and more to all increase as normal parts of your life as you follow Jesus and partner with Him in what He wants to do.

It doesn't really matter which day of the week you start reading this study, and there's no time like the present; so lets dig in!

SECTION 1:
Everybody Hears God

DAY 1
YOU WERE CREATED FOR THIS!

Art Thomas

Our natural habitat is in the presence of God. He made beasts of the field. He made birds of the air. He made fish and put them in the water. Then He made man and He stopped, and He said, "Let Us make man in Our image," and He breathed His breath into man. And that was our natural habitat — to be breathed-in by God. That's where we're supposed to stay always.

~ Scott Thompson

2 Corinthians 5:18-20 — All this is from God, who reconciled us to Himself through Christ and gave us the ministry of reconciliation: that God was reconciling the world to Himself in Christ, not counting people's sins against them. And He has committed to us the message of reconciliation. We are therefore Christ's ambassadors, as though God were making His appeal through us. We

implore you on Christ's behalf: Be
reconciled to God. (NIV)

YOU WERE CREATED TO HAVE A RELATIONSHIP WITH
God. That means hearing His voice will be the most
natural thing you will ever experience.

Many of us are waiting for the sky to rip open
and a voice to boom out of heaven. While God can,
in fact, do this (and has), it's an abnormal form of
communication for Him. Far more often, He speaks
to us in ways that don't feel supernatural at all.

That makes sense. You don't feel your own
skin unless something is wrong with it or you do
something intentional to it. That's because your skin
is always part of you. In the same way, God's voice
is intimately close to us at all times. You're
immersed in Him. You were physiologically
designed to interact with God — it's your first reason
for existence. Expect His voice to feel natural.

Whether or not you realize it, God has been
speaking to you for your entire life. He has been
reaching out to you through friends, family,
strangers, circumstances, and even your own
thoughts, feelings, dreams, and ideas.

Most importantly, He spoke two thousand
years ago through the life and ministry of His Son,
Jesus Christ.

When God originally created mankind, we
were designed inside of a loving relationship with
Him. But in order to keep us from being mindless
robots, He gave us a free will by offering a choice:
Remain in the life-giving relationship with Him for
which we were created, or live for ourselves — apart
from intimacy with Him — and die.

At its core, the word "sin" actually means to

"miss the mark." The only way to actually hit the "mark" of perfection is to fully trust the only One who is actually perfect (the One who purposely designed the target to be impossible to hit apart from trusting Him). Therefore, generally speaking, the actions we call "sins" are really just evidence that we didn't trust God in a given situation. Romans 14:23 says that "everything that does not come from faith [or active trust] is sin."

The relationship God originally designed for us to have with Him was not a long list of rules or a bunch of "dos and don'ts." You won't find that in the book of Genesis. Rather, it was a relational connection—a Father/child-type interaction where the only rule was to remain in humble, loving relationship with Him.

The first temptation in history questioned God's voice ("Did God really say...?") and caused the first man and woman to second-guess their trust of Him (Genesis 3:1). From the moment the first man and woman ate the forbidden fruit, all mankind defaulted to a broken relationship with the God who loves us. And God, recognizing that His most cherished creation had rebelled, immediately put His winning plan into action. He reached out mercifully to mankind, eventually sending His own Son to save us.

Jesus shed His blood on the cross as an outpouring of forgiveness toward mankind. He didn't sweep our sin under a cosmic rug and pretend it never happened. He entered into our pain, bore our sins in His body as He hung on the cross, and cancelled the curse of our separation from God.

When Jesus died, our sin died. Our old lives—ruled by sin—died with Him. What man was powerless to do, God did through the blood of Jesus. He saved us from eternal separation and made a way to truly know Him and interact with Him.

This incredible salvation is made freely available as a gracious gift. It's not something we can earn. Jesus already did everything that needed to be done.

There's only one stipulation: This free gift can only be experienced when we enter back into the humble, trust-filled relationship that God designed for us at the beginning of time. The Bible calls it "faith." Ephesians 2:8 clarifies that while it is indeed God's grace that saves us (and no work of our own), this free gift is only activated "through faith." It all boils down to trust. Do you trust that Jesus' sacrifice is enough to save you?

In a moment, you're going to receive an opportunity to respond to this message of hope. Whether you've been a Christian for years or whether you've never had a relationship with God, the following prayer time, Journal Experience, and Action Step are designed to lead you into a fresh encounter with the God who loves you.

God has been speaking to you for your entire life. At this moment, you may feel His presence like a warmth, a tingle, a stirring in the pit of your stomach, or electricity. Or you may feel nothing at all. Feelings are never the point; Jesus is. Whatever the case, God is speaking to you right now and beckoning you deeper into the relationship for which you were created.

Will you answer His invitation?

Prayer Starter:

❏ Thank God for sending Jesus to set you free from your old life of sin. Thank Him for being trustworthy, merciful, and good to you.

❏ Apologize for any lack of faith in your life that has led to sinful actions, and thank Jesus for freely forgiving you. Tell Him you receive His forgiveness and thank Him for it.

❏ Ask the Holy Spirit to transform you so that your entire life looks more like Jesus.

Journal Experience:

What is an area of your life where you have been trying to succeed in your own strength yet often miss the mark of heavenly perfection? (I'm not talking about being a perfectionist—I'm talking about expressing the beauty and excellence of heaven in the earth through partnership with Jesus). Perhaps it's something in the workplace, at home, at school, in your family, or maybe a matter of your overall salvation. If you feel there are multiple areas, just pick the one that is currently the most important to you and write it here:

_____

_____

_____

Ask the Holy Spirit to show you three specific ways

you can trust God more in that area of your life. Write down the solutions that come to mind.

_____

_____

_____

_____

_____

_____

_____

_____

_____

_____

_____

_____

_____

_____

_____

_____

_____

_____

_____

_____

Action Step:

James 2:17 tells us that "faith by itself, if it is not accompanied by action, is dead." If you are waiting until you have faith before you take action, it will never come. Faith only exists inside of trust-filled, obedient action. I like to say, "If you feel like your faith is dead, do something that requires faith. It will come alive!"

Today, put into action at least one of the three things you wrote down during the journal exercise.

Supplemental Reading:
- ❑ Genesis 2-3
- ❑ Romans 6
- ❑ Ephesians 2

DAY 2
THE DIFFERENCE BETWEEN
HEARING AND DISCERNING

James Loruss

I think a lot of times we think that we don't hear God, but we do hear God. And it takes a step of faith to realize we do hear God and to begin to trust that voice.

~ Audrey Aitken

1 Samuel 3:8-10 — A third time the Lord called, "Samuel!" And Samuel got up and went to Eli and said, "Here I am; you called me."

Then Eli realized that the Lord was calling the boy. So Eli told Samuel, "Go and lie down, and if He calls you, say, 'Speak, Lord, for Your servant is listening.'" So Samuel went and lay down in his place.

The Lord came and stood there, calling as at the other times, "Samuel! Samuel!"

> Then Samuel said, "Speak, for Your
> servant is listening." (NIV)

IN THIS PASSAGE, SAMUEL HAD AN ENCOUNTER WITH the voice of the Lord for the first time. In verse one of this chapter, it says, "In those days the word of the Lord was rare; there were not many visions," so we know hearing God's voice in Samuel's day was not normal.

The first time God called Samuel's name, his first reaction was to run to the nearest adult and say, "Here I am." This happened three times before Eli realized that this must be God speaking to the boy.

I find it interesting that Samuel heard God speak three times and mistook it for Eli's voice. Today, we might sit back and scoff at Samuel's ignorance with our Red Letter Edition and coffee in hand and think, *Geez, Samuel, get with it! I can understand missing it maybe once or twice, but three times? Really?* It's easy to give advice to someone when we already know the outcome. We need to remember, though, that at this time "Samuel did not yet know the Lord." Samuel had not yet learned what the voice of God sounded like. Who knows how long this would have gone on if it weren't for Eli's intervention!

It took Samuel four different times to hear God's voice, plus the discernment of someone else, for him to finally recognize the voice of God; but when He did recognize it, he responded with humility and obedience: "Speak, for Your servant is listening."

God is speaking to you and me each and every day. I wonder how often we miss His voice because we don't expect it or it's outside of our norm. It says in verse 2 that Eli's eyes were becoming weak so he could barely see. I'm sure it wasn't uncommon for Eli to call for Samuel, especially since he was losing his sight. Samuel probably assumed that Eli needed something like he had many nights before this. How many times do we go through our normal routine and mistake God's voice for something or someone else?

This happened in Jesus' day as well. As he was speaking to a crowd, "a voice came from heaven, 'I have glorified it, and will glorify it again.' The crowd that was there and heard it said it had thundered; others said an angel had spoken to him." (See John 12:28-29.) The whole crowd heard the exact same voice, yet many wrongly discerned it as an angel while others dismissed it as mere thunder. It is possible to hear God's voice yet fail to discern it.

Many times I have thought I was just hearing my own thoughts in my head, not realizing until later that it was actually God speaking to me. As Art said in the previous lesson, "You were physically designed to interact with God — it's your first reason for existence. Expect His voice to feel natural."

God is still speaking to us today, but we have the choice of whether or not to excuse it away. Although Samuel did not discern God's voice at first, he was willing and obedient and eventually recognized and believed God was speaking to him. We know from scripture that Samuel went on to do amazing things for the Lord and speak to the entire nation as a prophet, but it all started with discerning His voice and then following in obedience.

My prayer for you is that, like Samuel, you would remain open and obedient throughout this journey of discerning God's voice. Don't let the routines of life get in the way of recognizing what He's saying today. Expect to hear Him speak; and when you realize He may be speaking, turn your ear to the Lord and pay attention. Let your heart cry out along with Samuel: "Speak, Your servant is listening."

Prayer Starter:

- ❏ Thank God for speaking to you and for enabling you to hear Him.
- ❏ Ask God to search your heart and show you whether or not you have been obedient to the things He has already spoken to you—whether things He has said personally to you or things He has already said in Scripture.
- ❏ Ask God for a genuine encounter with Him and for clarity to discern His voice and obey. Ask God to teach you to pause and meditate when He does speak.

Journal Experience:

If possible, go to a quiet place that is free from distractions and busyness. Next, ask the Holy Spirit if there's anything He has been trying to show you that you haven't been discerning as His voice. He may speak that very thing to you, or He may alert you to a person or circumstance that He has been using to communicate. Simply write down whatever comes to mind. It will likely feel like your own thoughts, but don't worry about analyzing it until after you've written everything down. If not, ask Him if there's anything He would like to tell you today. Again, write down what comes to mind. After you're finished, you can take time to discern whether the thoughts that came to you were from God or not.

_____

_____

_____

_____

_____

_____

_____

_____

_____

_____

_____

_____

_____

_____

_____

_____

_____

_____

_____

_____

_____

_____

_____

_____

_____

_____

_____

_____

_____

_____

Action Step:

First, read over everything you wrote in today's journal experience. Now, think critically about everything you wrote. Is it compatible with what you know of the Bible? Does it seem to reflect the nature of Jesus (is it kind, merciful, compassionate, and liberating)?

Second, find a Christian who you trust, and tell them what you feel God spoke to you today. Ask them what they think and whether or not they feel like it came from God.

Supplemental Reading:
❑   John 10

DAY 3
EVERY CHRISTIAN HAS HEARD GOD'S VOICE

Art Thomas

You wouldn't be saved if you hadn't heard the voice of God — if you hadn't responded to the convicting presence of God...

~ Bill Hamon

> **John 6:44-45** — "No one can come to Me unless the Father who sent Me draws them, and I will raise them up at the last day. It is written in the Prophets: 'They will all be taught by God.' Everyone who has heard the Father and learned from Him comes to Me." (NIV)

IT SEEMS TO ME THAT NEARLY EVERYWHERE I GO, I can find Christians who say they've never heard God's voice. In reality, that's impossible! According to today's scripture, the only way to come to Jesus is to hear God's voice.

Now, before you start questioning your salvation, let me explain some specifics.

When you came to Jesus, chances are a loud voice never roared out of heaven at you. As we saw a couple days ago, since you were created for relationship with God, hearing God's voice is actually a very natural experience. And as you saw yesterday, it is possible to hear God's voice without realizing that it's Him.

Whether you became a Christian decades ago or even today, chances are something inside of you stirred when you heard the good news about Jesus. You felt an assurance deep inside that seemed to communicate something like, *This is right. I need to respond to this message. I need God in my life.*

That sensation — that conviction — was God's voice to you.

As you'll learn in later lessons, this certainly isn't the only way God speaks. It does, however, seem to be the most common. And even when God speaks in any of His other diverse ways, that inner clarity — that divine peace and assurance — still tends to be present to tip you off to the fact that what you're sensing is right and true.

In short, if you're a Christian, you're not allowed to say that you've never heard God's voice. What you can say — and what even the most seasoned minister will say (if they're honest) — is that you regularly *hear* God and are constantly learning to *discern* His voice with greater clarity and regularity.

You cannot separate the Christian life from communication with God because relationship with Him is the entire point of why He saved you.

Prayer Starter:

- ❑ Thank God for saving you and bringing you into a loving relationship with Him.
- ❑ Ask God to use this book to help you grow in hearing Him with more clarity.
- ❑ Thank the Holy Spirit for speaking to other people's hearts whenever you share the Good News with them. Ask Him to help you notice an opportunity this week to share His love with someone who needs to know Him.

Journal Experience:

The most powerful tool you have at your disposal is your own personal testimony. The heart of prophetic ministry is testifying about Jesus (Revelation 19:10).

Write down a short summary of your personal testimony below. First write one or two sentences about the person you once were and the lifestyle from which Jesus saved you. Then write one or two sentences about what God did to reach you that caused you to give your life to Jesus. Finally, write one or two sentences about the person you have become because of Jesus' work in you.

The Person You Used to Be:

_____

_____

_____

_____

_____

_____

_____

_____

What God Did to Reach You:

_____

_____

_____

_____

_____

_____

_____

_____

The Person You Are Now:

_____

_____

_____

_____

_____

_____

_____

Action Step:

The main point of today's lesson is to show you that you heard God's voice when someone shared the message of Jesus with you. That means that whenever you share your personal testimony with other people, you are creating a new opportunity for them to hear God's voice for themselves.

There's no pressure to know fancy theological terms or to have a bunch of Bible knowledge when you share your testimony. People can argue against ideas and doctrines, but they can't argue against your story. They either have to believe it or reject it as a lie. Your job is simply to share it with people.

Share your testimony with someone today. Ideally, share it with someone who isn't walking in a relationship with God; but if that's too intimidating for you right now, share your testimony instead with a fellow Christian to help you become more comfortable with telling your story.

You may find it helpful to say, "I'm trying to learn how to tell my life story in under two minutes. Do you mind if I practice on you?" Or you may simply find that God opens a door for you to share your story naturally in a conversation. Keep your eyes open for an opportunity, and don't be afraid to make one yourself.

Supplemental Reading:
❑   Revelation 12:10-12, especially verse 11

DAY 4
KNOWING THE SHEPHERD

James Loruss

He's a speaking God, and we have ears to hear. He says that 'My sheep know My voice.' ...God has expressed Himself in a desire to talk with His people. He loves His people, and He created us for the purpose of loving Him.
~ Wayne Benson

> **John 10:27** — My sheep listen to My voice; I know them, and they follow Me. (NIV)

EVERYTHING BEGINS AND ENDS WITH KNOWING Jesus. Without Him, everything else becomes meaningless. You can desire to have an effective ministry or to do amazing things for God, but these things must flow from knowing the Shepherd.

I want Jesus to know every part of me. It's all about relationship! If you do ministry for any other reason than out of love for Jesus, then you've missed it. We do ministry because we love Jesus. It's out of love. Ministry should flow out of relationship, not duty.

Remember what Jesus said in Matthew 7:21-23: "Not everyone who says to Me, 'Lord, Lord,' will enter the kingdom of heaven, but only the one who does the will of My Father who is in heaven. Many will say to Me on that day, 'Lord, Lord, did we not prophesy in Your name and in Your name drive out demons and in Your name perform many miracles?' Then I will tell them plainly, 'I never knew you. Away from Me, you evildoers!'"

Ouch.

It's not enough just to hear His voice and prophesy — we need to be known by Him. Notice how Paul hints at this principle: "But now that you know God — or rather are known by God..." (Galatians 4:9). Paul indicates that God knowing us is even more important than us knowing God. First Corinthians 8:3 teaches, "But whoever loves God is known by God." It all starts when we open up our hearts and become vulnerable with the One we love.

Love leads to intimacy. Love also leads to obedience. Jesus said, "My sheep listen to My voice," and continued, "I know them, *and* they follow Me." In John 14:23, Jesus said, "Anyone who loves Me will obey my teaching." Love is the connection with Jesus that opens our hearts to Him. It is the gateway to heartfelt obedience and a successful Christian life.

Christianity is as much about Jesus knowing you as it is about you knowing Him. Jesus is inviting you deeper into a real and authentic relationship with Him.

Prayer Starter:

- ❑ Focus your heart on Jesus and thank Him for being your Shepherd. Thank Him for His sacrifice and the simple joy of knowing Him.
- ❑ If you've been distracted with anything else than knowing Jesus, repent and receive God's forgiveness.
- ❑ Ask Jesus to reveal His heart through you today as you focus on His love for yourself and for others.

Journal Experience:

Ask Jesus if there has been anything you have been believing about Him that isn't true. Write down the first thing that comes to mind. If the thing that comes to mind is something you don't technically believe in intellectually, write it down anyway. You may find that your heart has led you to live contrary to your theology, and Jesus is showing you that you aren't actually living as though what you believe is true.

_____

_____

_____

_____

_____

_____

_____

Second, pray, "Jesus, I give to You this lie that I have believed. What do You want to give me in return?" Write down whatever comes to mind. It may be words, a picture, or some other feeling. If it's symbolic, first write the symbol and then your interpretation of what it might mean. Again, go with the first thing that comes to you.

_____

_____

_____

_____

_____

Finally, ask Him, "Jesus, what do You think of me?" Write down the thoughts that come to mind.

_____

_____

_____

_____

_____

_____

_____

_____

_____

_____

_____

_____

_____

_____

_____

_____

_____

_____

_____

_____

_____

_____

Action Step:

Ask Jesus what He thinks about someone you know. Bear in mind that when God speaks to us about other people, His goal is always to strengthen, encourage, and comfort that person (1 Corinthians 14:3).

_____

_____

_____

_____

_____

_____

_____

_____

_____

_____

_____

_____

_____

_____

_____

_____

_____

_____

If what you wrote down does not seem encouraging, ask the Lord if it truly was Him. If you still feel it may have been God, ask Him how to use the information in a way that strengthens, encourages, and comforts the person.

Finally, write a note (or e-mail, text message, Facebook message, etc.) to the person. Let them know, "I was praying for you, and I felt like God might be saying this about you..." You may want to tell them that you're learning to hear God's voice, and ask them to give you feedback and to let you know how it made them feel or what it meant to them.

Supplemental Reading:
❑ Psalm 23
❑ Proverbs 8:17

DAY 5
YOU MAY ALL PROPHESY

Jonathan Ammon

The prophetic is a big deal. Everyone has the privilege of prophesying. Everyone has the privilege. Really what it is is hearing from God and speaking. That's all it is.

~ *Bill Johnson*

> 1 **Corinthians 14:31** — For you can all prophesy in turn so that everyone may be instructed and encouraged. (NIV)

IN NUMBERS 11, MOSES MUST DEAL WITH THE PEOPLE of Israel complaining about their diet and the Lord's provision for what must have seemed like the umpteenth time. Part of the solution involved gathering the seventy elders that Moses had appointed to help him lead. These elders gathered around the tabernacle, and God placed His Spirit upon them. They began to prophesy. It must have been holy chaos. Seventy men who had never experienced the Holy Spirit upon them suddenly received the words of God. Moses's protégé, Joshua, was upset and told Moses to stop them. Joshua thought that only Moses, the prophet and leader, could prophesy. Moses reflected the heart of God when he replied, "Oh, that all the Lord's people were prophets and that the Lord would put His Spirit upon them!" (Numbers 11:29). Moses expressed the desire and plan of God to be accomplished centuries later in a New Covenant.

When God poured out His Spirit on the day of Pentecost, He fulfilled the words of the prophet Joel: "I will pour out My Spirit on all flesh, and your sons and your daughters shall prophesy" (Acts 2:16-17 NKJV). The empowerment of the Spirit was poured out and made available to all.

We all were given access to the Spirit and His gifts. To qualify for spiritual gifts—and specifically for prophecy—we need only to be "sons and daughters" and receive the gift that God has poured out. When God's Spirit rests upon you, this is as simple as believing the truth that you can prophesy. In fact, if you have been following the action steps in this book, you already have. You have listened to what God is saying and told someone else for their encouragement. That is prophecy (1 Corinthians 14:3).

Scripture plainly states that every single person has the ability to prophesy. It is available to all for the purpose of instructing and encouraging others.

Paul commands the Corinthians to "desire spiritual gifts, but especially that you may prophesy" (1 Corinthians 14:1, NKJV). Every single one of us must have an earnest desire to prophesy. But without the belief that we can, that desire is hollow. Paul goes on to describe what prophecy is, "he who prophesies speaks edification and exhortation and comfort to men" (1 Corinthians 14:3, NKJV). To prophesy is to say what God is saying, and this results in encouragement and building up. Paul emphasizes this gift to the Corinthians and explicitly states that it is available to every single believer (1 Corinthians 14:31).

If I were to ask a room full of people to draw their house, every single person could attempt the assignment. Almost everyone could draw a box with a triangle on top and a little window. But if I looked around the room I could probably identify some people who had a gift. Maybe they drew a beautiful, accurate picture of the house they live in. This artistic gift demonstrates both talent and skill, as all talents must be developed. There may be a more artistically gifted person who spent less time developing their gift who drew something less impressive. But regardless of talent or skill, every single person has the basic ability to represent their house with lines on a piece of paper.

Similarly, you can all prophesy. Some may be gifted. Some may have spent more time developing that gift. But every single person can say what God is saying in any given moment by the will and the supernatural ability of the Spirit. This is God's desire and heart for His people. It is part of His covenant and His relationship with us, and it is part of our inheritance as sons and daughters of God. Regardless of who you've been, what you've done, how smart you are, how long you've been a believer, or what you are struggling with today, you can prophesy. It is in God's covenant and promise for you.

Prayer Starter:

- ❑ Thank God for the gift of prophecy that He has given to the body of Christ. Thank God that He has given you the ability to prophesy.
- ❑ Tell God that you earnestly desire to prophesy, express your faith that you can with His help.
- ❑ Thank God for the encouraging effect of prophecy and for the promise that He will use you to bless and encourage others as He speaks through you.

Journal Experience:

What do you feel is the most intimidating part of being a spokesperson for God?

_____

_____

_____

Ask the Father to tell you something He knows that will help you overcome any fear or intimidation attached to the above issue. Write down whatever comes to mind.

_____

_____

_____

_____

_____

_____

_____

_____

_____

_____

_____

_____

_____

_____

Action Step:

Find a Christian friend who you trust. Tell them that you're learning to hear God's voice, and ask if you can practice on them.

When you find someone who is willing to let you practice, pray out loud and ask, "God, please tell me one of the wonderful thoughts You have about [person's name]." Then wait.

Psalm 139:18 says that God's thoughts about each of us outnumber the sands on the seashore. It isn't hard to find a grain of sand on the beach! And Jeremiah 33:3 teaches us that God answers those who call to Him, and He will reveal "great and unsearchable things" that we don't already know.

When you pray and wait, what you sense may come in the form of words, a picture, a feeling, or vague thoughts. First Corinthians 2:16 tells us that "we have the mind of Christ," so even if it feels like your own thoughts, give it a shot anyway because God may indeed be speaking to you. Whatever method God uses to communicate, trust that it's Him, and humbly share what you think you're discerning. Be open and honest about the growth process, and feel free to use disarming phrases like, "I think God might be saying..." or, "I'm not sure about this, but here's the picture that came to my mind..."

Don't worry about how much detail you're sharing; just be faithful to share what comes to you that you feel may be God. Romans 12:6 says that we should prophesy in proportion to our faith. So if you're not yet comfortable sharing specific details (or if you aren't sensing any), there's no pressure to do so. Faith comes through hearing what God is saying.

Finally, ask the person if they found the message you shared to be encouraging or comforting. If you thought you were sensing specific information, ask them if what you said was true.

SECTION 2:
Some of the Ways God Speaks

DAY 6
THE STILL, SMALL VOICE

Jonathan Ammon

God's voice is seldom a voice. More often than not it's an impression; it's a thought...

~ Steve Thompson

> **1 Kings 19:11-13** — Then He said, "Go out, and stand on the mountain before the Lord." And behold, the Lord passed by, and a great and strong wind tore into the mountains and broke the rocks in pieces before the Lord, but the Lord was not in the wind; and after the wind an earthquake, but the Lord was not in the earthquake; and after the earthquake a fire, but the Lord was not in the fire; and after the fire a still small voice.
>
> So it was, when Elijah heard it, that he wrapped his face in his mantle and went out and stood in the entrance of the cave. Suddenly a voice came to him,

and said, "What are you doing here, Elijah?" (NKJV)

I WAS DRIVING BACK TO DETROIT, MICHIGAN, FROM Pennsylvania when nature began to call, and I decided to stop for gas and the restroom. I parked my car and walked into the highway rest stop. I entered the public restroom, and a young man in a white t-shirt exited. As I walked past him, I immediately had the thought, *Share the Gospel with him*.

I was caught off-guard. I would have to spin around and chase him down to share the Gospel with him (and I wasn't entirely sure that this wasn't just my own thoughts telling me I needed to share the Gospel with everyone). I prayed a quick prayer that if that small thought was really God, I would be able to meet this guy again somehow.

A couple of hours later, again on the highway, another small thought came to me: *Pull off at this rest stop*. I checked my gas gauge, and I didn't need gas. I didn't have to go to the bathroom. I wanted to get home, but I thought to myself, *Who knows; maybe it is God*. I pulled off at the rest stop.

I parked and got out of my car, and a voice behind me said,

"Hey! I saw you at the last rest stop!" I turned around, and it was the young man in the white t-shirt who I had felt I needed to share the Gospel with. God had answered my prayer and given me another opportunity! I was able to share God's love for him and found out that he had packed up everything and was moving across the country on a whim to start a new life. I told him that he could start a new life with Jesus.

Both times that God spoke to me, it was in what we usually identify as "a still, small voice." I've heard this described as "a quiet whisper," "a thought in your heart," or sometimes "a small thought on the edge of your mind." It is not an overwhelming voice or phenomenon. In fact, it is often so simple and ordinary that we mistake it for our own thoughts. It is not conspicuous.

First Kings 19:11-13 recounts numerous attention-getting events and manifestations, but none of them were God — a whirlwind, an earthquake, and a fire. Sometimes I think that if these things happened today, we would place some kind of meaning on them. The Bible clearly states that God was not in them. God was in the still small voice. It was quiet. It was not attention-grabbing. It did not demand notice. It was there for the one who was listening. When Elijah heard it, he went out to meet with God. The still, small voice was an invitation to come and hear.

I hear God in a still, small voice perhaps more than any other way. Like my experience on the highway, we have a choice of whether or not we will listen. As small and perhaps humble as the voice is, will we turn aside to pay attention? When Elijah did he entered into a conversation with God.

When we are listening for God's voice, we must be aware of the small thoughts, the low whispers, the still voice that invites us to listen and discover God speaking. It may seem like our own thoughts. It may not seem impressive, but it leads into communion with God.

In the same way that God chose to enter humanity as a baby in a small town in a small nation, God often chooses to enter conversation with us in small ways. He invites us to investigate—to turn aside and listen.

Prayer Starter:

❑ Thank God for choosing to relate to us in small ways. Ask Him to tune you to when He speaks in a still, small voice.

❑ Is there anything you have recently heard as "a still, small voice," "a thought in your heart," "a whisper in your mind?" Ask God to remind you of anything that He was speaking to you this way that you may have missed.

❑ Ask God to help you be aware of His voice in small situations when you are out among people. Ask Him to help you hear the "still, small voice" even in the midst of other conversation.

Journal Experience:

Has God ever spoken to you in a still, small voice? What did it sound like? What did it feel like? What was the result? Did the still, small voice lead to greater revelation? Write some reflections about your experience(s) that answer these questions.

_____

_____

_____

_____

_____

_____

_____

_____

_____

_____

_____

_____

_____

_____

_____

_____

_____

Action Step:

Ask God to speak to you in "a still, small voice" this week. Grab a small notebook and keep it handy. Whenever something that may be God's "still, small voice" comes to your mind, write it down and investigate if it is God speaking.

Supplemental Reading:
❏ Zechariah 4:6
❏ Job 4:16

DAY 7
EXTERNAL WAYS GOD SPEAKS

James Loruss

One night I was laying on my car windshield outside and looking up at the stars. I thought, "God, if You're there, would You just let a shooting star go by?" Boom. Shooting star. And I just thought that was so weird. "Okay — that probably wasn't You, Lord... Would You do another shooting star?" And I just sat out there for an hour watching one after another, after another.

~ Lacey Thompson

Romans 1:20 — For since the creation of the world God's invisible qualities—His eternal power and divine nature—have been clearly seen, being understood from what has been made, so that people are without excuse. (NIV)

Hebrews 2:3b-4 — This salvation, which was first announced by the Lord, was confirmed to us by those who heard Him.

God also testified to it by signs, wonders and various miracles, and by gifts of the Holy Spirit distributed according to His will. (NIV)

Hebrews 12:7 — Endure hardship as discipline; God is treating you as His children. For what children are not disciplined by their father? (NIV)

I'M SURE YOU'VE HEARD PEOPLE SAY, 'ACTIONS speak louder than words'. I believe that this is a heavenly principle. God is a God of action. He doesn't just say, "I love you" — He shows it. He isn't just Creator by name — He creates! When God speaks, something happens. His voice is an action in itself. God's first interaction with His creation was through His voice. "Let there be..." and it was made. (See Genesis 1.)

Think of any good painter or artist. What is their greatest desire when trying to create a masterpiece? To express what is in their heart on a page or canvas — often to make the viewer feel the very same thing. Where do we think this desire came from? Is that not God's intention when He created everything in nature?

I believe it is the desire of every human heart to seek and find beauty and then celebrate it, just like our Creator. Colossians 1:15-17 says, "The Son is the image of the invisible God, the firstborn over all creation. For in Him all things were created: things in heaven and on earth, visible and invisible, whether thrones or powers or rulers or authorities; all things have been created through Him and for Him. He is before all things, and in Him all things hold together." Everything was created through Jesus and for Jesus. He designed creation to be a testimony of His character. Jeremiah 10:12 says that the Lord "made the earth by His power; He founded the world by His wisdom and stretched out the heavens by His understanding."

> His power made the earth.
> His wisdom founded the world.
> His understanding stretched the heavens.

God not only shows His love for us through nature but through signs and wonders and special moments tailored just for you to catch your attention and draw you close. He is intentional and specific.

I remember being a counselor at a summer camp for boys and girls in the foster care system. There was one little boy in my group we'll call "Joe." He was an incredibly sweet kid and always had a smile on his face. I remember asking my campers what they were looking forward to that week. Joe spoke up and said in a quiet yet confident voice, "I want an arrow because I want to be like Daniel Boone." How an arrow makes you like Daniel Boone is beyond me, but nonetheless that was his wish. I remember saying, "Let's pray that God would you help you, and maybe you'll find an arrow this week."

Now this may not seem like a big deal to you, but these kids from the foster system are used to disappointment. They have typically been abused, neglected, or abandoned. Whether I was right or not to say this, I put God's good name out there, and now it was His job to confirm it.

The next day while the boys were looking for bugs, suddenly I heard Joe squealing with excitement, "Look what I found!"

It was an arrow!

Impossibly, he had found it buried underneath the grass near a tree. I couldn't believe it! I then said, "Joe, this is a sign that God loves you, buddy. He helped you find this arrow because He knew it meant something to you." I was then able to share more with him about God's love through His Son, Jesus.

Call it coincidence or happenstance; I call it the love of my Father.

God confirms His love in many ways. Yes, Jesus paying for our sins on the cross is the only proof we should ever need, but what good father merely says, "I love you," once? God continues to confirm His love through signs and wonders. Don't be afraid to tell people what God is capable of doing. God is speaking, and He wants to use you to make His voice known.

When someone experiences the power of God in an external way, they are experiencing His voice in action. His actions are backed by His voice, and His voice reveals His heart for humanity. He will do whatever it takes to know us and be known by us. Whether it's a breathtaking scene in nature or a hidden arrow under a tree, God will do whatever it takes to say, "I love you."

Prayer Starter:

- ❑ Thank God that His heart and character are clearly revealed through all of His creation.
- ❑ Praise Him and celebrate in the truth that you are created in His image.
- ❑ Ask God to give you an opportunity to point at creation as a witness of His love for someone.

Journal Experience:

Choose an item from nature (even better if you can walk outside, find that item, and actually handle it). As you read in today's first scripture, Romans 1:20, we see that God has revealed His invisible attributes through the things He has made. Ask the Holy Spirit how the piece of nature you chose reveals God. Write down the item you chose and then the thoughts that come to you about how that item reveals God.

_____

_____

_____

_____

_____

_____

_____

_____

_____

_____

_____

_____

_____

_____

_____

_____

_____

_____

_____

Action Step:

Share a message of God's love today with someone using an item from nature. You can use the item that you already found for your own experience or you can choose to find a new one. You might begin the conversation with something like, "I had this crazy thought today when I saw _____..." or, "Have you ever thought about ____? It makes me realize that God is like _____..."

Supplemental Reading:
❑ Genesis 1
❑ Psalm 19:1-6

DAY 8
IMPRESSIONS AND SENSATIONS

Art Thomas

For me, it is generally God moving in my passions. There is normally a burden that is accompanying it… Maybe I'm just an emotional guy, but that seems to be how it works for me. I start to get kind of a heartbrokenness for the issue…

~ J.P. Dorsey

> **Acts 27:9b-10** — …Paul advised them, saying, "Men, I perceive that this voyage will end with disaster and much loss, not only of the cargo and ship, but also our lives." (NKJV)

HAVE YOU EVER HAD A FEELING LIKE SOMETHING bad was about to happen, and then it did? What about waking up and feeling like God was going to do something awesome that day, and then He came through?

Sensations, perceptions, and subtle impressions are all ways in which God sometimes speaks to us.

I am frequently invited to speak at conferences and to train churches in healing ministry. Occasionally I will feel a subtle warmth, tingle, or even just an awareness of some area on my body, and I'll know God is directing me to minister healing ministry to someone who has a problem in that same area. I'm not hearing clear words. I'm not even always certain that it's God. But fairly consistently, when I respond to these sensations and ask if someone in the room is suffering in that way, we see a miracle happen that builds everyone's faith.

In today's scripture, we see that Paul perceived danger and great loss to the ship and crew, but they didn't heed his warning. Sure enough, that voyage ended in shipwreck. Sometimes God will utilize the glands in our bodies to trigger a "danger" response that almost feels like instinct. In this way He can spare our lives or the lives of others.

Some of us, however, have overactive imaginations and a low threshold for irrational fears. If it is our normal personality to be nervous about anything new, and if we are regularly given to apprehension and distrust, then it is going to be very difficult to discern when God is speaking to us in this subtle way. For this reason, we need to learn to trust God and allow His boundless love to eradicate fear from our lives. The more consistently peaceful we are — physically, emotionally, psychologically, and spiritually — the more easily we will be able to discern out-of-the-ordinary impressions and sensations from the Lord.

I remember a period of three or four months

where I kept thinking I was having "words of knowledge" that people around me had a problem in their right knee. Ninety-five percent of the time, they told me their knee was fine. Suddenly it occurred to me that maybe these feelings weren't God, and I actually had a problem with my own knee! I started exercising my legs and stretching regularly. Then I noticed the recurring sensations in my knee stopped.

A few months later, I was talking to a pastor and felt something in my right knee. This time I knew it wasn't me because I had been taking care of my knee's health. The regular sensations I used to have no longer occurred. When I asked the Lord if this feeling was Him, He gave me a little more information. I suddenly somehow "knew" an extra detail. I asked the man, "Do you have an old football injury in your right knee that still gives you trouble?" The pastor was shocked. It was true. I laid hands on his knee, had him test it out, and all the pain instantly left.

As we quiet ourselves internally, walk in the peace of God, and take care of our physical health, we become better receptors for the subtle ways God speaks.

Prayer Starter:

- ❑ Thank God that you are "fearfully and wonderfully made." Thank Him for designing your body in such a way that He can communicate with you in these ways.
- ❑ Ask the Lord to help you discern the moments when He is speaking to you in subtle ways so that you can be a help to others.
- ❑ Ask the Holy Spirit for boldness to share with others what you think you're perceiving whenever God speaks.

Journal Experience:

Ask God if there are any areas of your life that are causing unnecessary "noise" and making it difficult to discern His subtle impressions. This "noise" could be something physical like my knee, or it could be emotional patterns, psychological concerns, or spiritual turmoil. For each thing God shows you, ask Him what He wants you to do to bring health and peace to that area of your life.

_____

_____

_____

_____

_____

_____

_____

_____

_____

_____

_____

_____

_____

_____

_____

_____

_____

_____

_____

_____

Action Step:

After completing the above Journal Experience, tell a Christian friend you trust the things God showed you that need to change. Together, determine some reasonable "first steps" toward implementing the things He told you to do. If they can't be done immediately, set some achievable dates as goals. Ask your friend to keep you accountable in following through on those things.

Day 9
Visions and Dreams

Art Thomas

Dreams are a big one. It's at night when we sleep and we get out of the way enough, and then God can speak to us. And He speaks to us through funny ways. Don't just get the dream and go, "Ok, that was a weird dream." Get the dream and ask God, "God, were You speaking in this dream? What were You trying to say?"

~ Scott Thompson

Job 33:14-15 — For God does speak—now one way, now another—though no one perceives it. In a dream, in a vision of the night, when deep sleep falls on people as they slumber in their beds. (NIV)

Joel 2:28b — ...Your sons and daughters will prophesy, your old men will dream dreams, your young men will see visions. (NIV)

JEREMIAH 23:16 TELLS US THAT TRUE VISIONS COME "from the mouth of the Lord." God often speaks in pictures. Sometimes those pictures are literal, and sometimes they're figurative. Either way, if it came from God, it's because He is trying to communicate with you.

While the Bible doesn't break things down quite this far, experience shows that there are basically three different types of visions: (1) visions in the night (more commonly called "dreams"), (2) open visions (seen while awake, somehow taking place in the visual field in front of your eyes), and (3) closed visions (being "seen" as mental pictures within the visual center of your mind).

Joel's prophecy (Joel 2:28) shows that visions and dreams are to be common experiences for both young and old alike. While God does indeed speak to different people in different ways, dreams and visions are some of the most common—first, because they're biblically for everyone and, second, because a picture can convey so much information so quickly. As the old saying goes, "A picture is worth a thousand words."

In one of my small group meetings a couple years ago, I set out a couple small tables in the middle of the room, each with a brightly-colored gift bag on top. On one table, next to the gift bag sat a picture of a dog and a die from a board game, turned up to the number one. On the other table, next to the gift bag sat a toy racecar and a die turned up to the number two.

I told those present that they—as a group— needed to choose one bag, and they would all be able to share and enjoy the contents of that bag.

One asked me, "Are we allowed to ask

questions?"

"Absolutely," I answered.

"Do the items on the outside of the bag have anything to do with what's inside?"

"Yes."

The group deliberated for some time until finally they arrived at the conclusion that "racecars are cooler than dogs" and chose bag number two.

I reached into the bag and offered everyone the contents to share: a box of laxatives.

"What was in the other bag?" they demanded.

I pulled out a package of full-size Snickers candy bars.

"What did the things outside the bags mean?" they asked.

I pointed to the first bag and said, "The dog in this picture is our pastor's dog, named 'Snickers.' And the die is turned to number 'one' because if you choose this bag, then you've 'won' Snickers!"

"What about the bag with the racecar?"

"Easy," I replied, holding up the die turned to the number two. "This bag will make you go 'number two'..." then lifting the racecar, "...really fast."

The laughter lasted only as long as it took for someone to say, "That's not fair! How were we supposed to know any of that?"

I smiled and replied, "You could have asked me. You knew you were allowed to ask questions. If you had asked me what the symbols meant, I would have told you." I then taught the group about when God sometimes speaks to us in visions and dreams with strange symbols.

Whenever God speaks in a strange symbol,

He's not doing it so that we will ask all our friends what they think it means. Neither is He doing it so that we will run to our "dream interpretation manual" that we purchased and keep on the bookshelf (my apologies to anyone who has written such a book). When God speaks in symbols, He is inviting us into a dialogue through which He will reveal the meaning.

Typically, the language He uses in the vision or dream is something that will make sense to us (either at face value or after a little interaction with Him). Other times, the imagery He uses will make sense to the person to whom you're ministering. But at no point does He intend for you to try to figure it out apart from Him. If you will dialogue with Him, He will reveal the meaning.

Dreams happen when you're sleeping — typically at night, but arguably any time of the day that you might happen to doze off. God uses these times to speak to us while our conscious minds are at rest, often giving us a more straightforward message than He can convey when our conscious minds are actively analyzing everything we see as we see it. Not every dream comes from God — some are inspired by entertainment we've been watching, family problems, unresolved fears, or just eating something funky. But many do come from the Lord. A good practice is that whenever you can remember a dream, ask the Lord if it was from Him. If you feel that it was, write down every detail you can remember, and only then start asking about the meaning (otherwise it's too easy to forget the details).

Open visions can take on a few forms. One is when you see the spiritual realm around you with your physical eyes (as in 2 Kings 6:15-17). Similarly, many people see (or perhaps a better word is "discern") the spiritual realm around them with their spiritual eyes—not physically seeing what's happening, yet still having a spiritual awareness that is so real that the things "seen" may as well be visible. Some ministers (myself included) have spiritually "seen" a word or two floating over a person's head. Others have reported visions that "looked as though a movie screen opened up in front of my eyes." If God is speaking visually to you, and what you're seeing is somehow viewed in the world around you (whether with natural eyes or spiritual eyes), you're seeing an open vision.

Closed visions, on the other hand, while also pictorial in nature, happen within your mind (not in your field of view). We tend to understand the word "imagination." If I say, "Imagine a pencil," you can "see" a pencil in your mind without seeing it in front of your eyes. That's the part of your brain that God gave you so that He can speak to you in pictures. Some things we see in our minds are our imagination while other things are placed there deliberately by God as a form of communication. If I'm praying for someone and a random picture comes into my imagination, there's a very good chance that this picture came from God. This is a closed vision.

No matter what you see—whether in a dream, an open vision, or a closed vision—ask God about it. It may appear literal at first glance and yet be figurative. I even once had something appear figurative that turned out to be literal.

If I'm ministering to someone when a vision comes, sometimes I tell the person what I see, and then I ask if it means anything to them. Most of the time it doesn't, but this is one way I go out on a limb and activate my faith. Once I've spoken it out loud, I can't really escape the fact that it happened, and I am forced to humble myself in front of the person and ask, "Okay, Lord, what did You mean by that?" The other benefit of doing things this way is that it allows me a way to break from the discussion or prayer and listen to the Lord without distraction for a moment. When the person hears you ask God for insight out loud, they're generally patient and grant you the liberty to briefly close your eyes in silence.

You can see visions. You can dream dreams. Pay attention to the things you perceive in your spirit and in your mind. The more you practice with what you see, the more easily you'll be able to identify when God is speaking to you in this way.

Prayer Starter:

- ❑ Read John 14:19-21. Ask Jesus to give you visions and dreams of Him.
- ❑ Ask God to help you recognize when He's speaking to you through a vision or a dream and to help you interpret what He is saying.
- ❑ Ask the Holy Spirit to give you visions when you're ministering to other people or praying for them.

Journal Experience:

Ask Jesus to tell you what He sees when He looks at you. Whether He answers in pictures or words, write down the thoughts and impressions that come to you.

_____

_____

_____

_____

_____

_____

_____

_____

_____

_____

_____

_____

_____

_____

_____

_____

_____

_____

_____

_____

When you're done, read what you wrote and take time to discern whether each thing you wrote sounds like your loving God.

Action Step:

I don't believe in forcing God to speak a certain way (that's an easy way to slip into deception as we look for any spirit that will speak to us in the way we are requiring). However, I do believe in exercising your imagination! As Mark Virkler said in our interview with him, "If you're allowed to think your theology, then you're also allowed to picture your theology."

I also believe in maintaining a holy imagination, which means that it is set apart for special and valuable service to God. This requires that you make every effort to stop using your imagination to imagine sin and instead use your imagination to imagine good things. In Romans 6:13, Paul said, "Do not offer any part of yourself to sin as an instrument of wickedness, but rather offer yourselves to God as those who have been brought from death to life; and offer every part of yourself to him as an instrument of righteousness." Your spirit, your brain, and therefore your imagination are all parts of you that need to be set apart for God's use.

Jesus said that if you look at a woman lustfully, it's the same as actually committing adultery (Matthew 5:28). If thinking intently about sin affects your relationship with God the same as actually committing that sin, then it stands to reason that thinking intently about righteous living will affect your relationship with God positively.

Take a couple minutes to imagine yourself ministering to someone you know — perhaps prophesying over them or successfully ministering healing to them. Allow yourself to imagine the best-case-scenario. And when you're done, ask God to give you experiences like the one you imagined.

Supplemental Reading:
As you read the following passages, allow yourself to imagine what it must have looked like to the author. Use your imagination for a holy purpose!

- ❑ Isaiah 6:1-8
- ❑ Daniel 7:9-10
- ❑ Revelation 4
- ❑ Revelation 20:11-15

DAY 10
UNUSUAL WAYS GOD SPEAKS

Art Thomas

He wants to talk to us so much and so badly that He'll use anything.

~ Tom Roan

Numbers 12:6-8a — [God] said, "Listen to My words: When there is a prophet among you, I, the Lord, reveal Myself to them in visions, I speak to them in dreams. But this is not true of My servant Moses; he is faithful in all My house. With him I speak face to face, clearly and not in riddles; he sees the form of the Lord... (NIV)

Acts 10:10 — [Peter] became hungry and wanted something to eat, and while the meal was being prepared, he fell into a trance. (NIV)

I HAVE BEEN BLESSED TO EXPERIENCE A SMALL handful of God-initiated trances and profound "divine encounters." In every case, I absolutely needed God to speak to me in such a clear way in order to capture my attention and assure me that I was truly interacting with Him.

Before I explain trances and divine encounters, I want to offer a context for such experiences. I know many people who wish they had experiences like I've had. They want to see the face of Jesus or interact with Him in undeniable ways. But I have come to a realization that I feel is valuable in the Body of Christ.

After rising from the dead, Jesus let Thomas touch the holes where the nails and spear had pierced Him. Then He said, "Because you have seen Me, you have believed; blessed are those who have not seen and yet have believed" (John 20:29).

There is a blessing attached to believing without seeing. Jesus didn't rebuke Thomas for needing to see, but He did let him know that he missed out on the blessing that comes from belief without sight.

God will always speak as loudly as He needs to in order for us to hear Him, but He prefers not to rob us of the blessing of believing without seeing. Therefore, whenever God speaks, He does so in a way that still requires faith to respond.

In other words, I believe the reason God has given me such clear encounters with Him is actually that my faith was weak, and He couldn't get through to me any other way. No disciples other than "doubting Thomas" were invited to touch Jesus' scars. I wish my faith was strong enough to have believed what God was trying to say without needing Him to put me into a trance or appear to me in an open vision.

When God put Peter into a trance in Acts 10, it was because He knew it was the only way to open Peter's mind to sharing the Gospel with people who weren't Jews. And we know Peter had a thick head about this issue because Paul later had to publicly rebuke him for distancing himself from Gentile Christians. (See Galatians 2:11-21.)

In the Old Testament, Moses had responsibility for leading all the people of God from Egypt to the Promised Land. There was no room for error. So God led them in very physical ways—a cloud by day and a pillar of fire by night. And He spoke to Moses in the clearest ways possible— appearing to him face-to-face and even writing His commands on stone Himself. If it hadn't been for God's clarity with Moses, the people might have died in the wilderness (making God a liar, which He is certainly not). The greater the risk involved with our failure, the more clearly God reveals His instructions.

Many Christians have treated such clear visions and encounters as badges of honor, as though such experiences validated their ministries or made them better Christians than everyone else. But speaking as one who has had such encounters, I would argue that it's really a sign of my weakness— that God needed to use such extreme measures to get through my thick head.

In other words, if you never have encounters like these, don't feel bad. God is allowing you to enjoy the blessing of believing without seeing. And it might even be a sign that you have greater faith than I do!

With all that said, there is no reason not to

desire such encounters with God. In every case where I have had such an experience, I was already actively engaged in prayer, hungering for God to speak to me. While a couple of Moses' encounters were initiated by God (the burning bush and the burning mountain, for example), the most common face-to-face encounters Moses had with God were when he traveled a half-mile outside the Israelite camp to spend time in the "Tent of Meeting."

If you want intense encounters with God, then you desire a good thing. The question is how much you want these encounters. Are you willing to set aside all distractions and spend time alone with God in expectation? And if you are, how long are you willing to wait? If He doesn't reveal Himself powerfully to you within the first ten times you try to meet with Him, will you give up? Or will you continue to pursue the One who has so faithfully pursued you?

Prayer Starter:

- ❑ Ask God for powerful encounters with Him. Ask Him to reveal Himself to you in new and exciting ways.
- ❑ Tell the Lord why you want to meet with Him in a more profound way. Explain what it would mean to your heart and how it would affect your walk with Him and your actions.
- ❑ Ask God to make you into the type of person through whom other people can encounter Him. Ask Him for integrity and consistency in your life as you reveal Jesus to a world that isn't fully experiencing Him.

Journal Experience:

Ask the Holy Spirit if you have any fears in your heart about being in God's presence. If you realize that you do, ask Him what truth God wants you to believe about Him, and write down what He shares with you. If you feel that you don't have any such fears, ask God to tell you why He wants to spend time with you, and write down what comes to mind.

_____

_____

_____

_____

_____

_____

_____

_____

_____

_____

_____

_____

_____

_____

_____

_____

_____

Action Step:

Christian trances are not self-induced. They are God-induced. New Age cults and Eastern religions practice a counterfeit of trances that involves emptying yourself or achieving an altered state of consciousness through self-will. In contrast, Christian trances are initiated by God, usually when we least expect it.

For this reason, your action step today will not be to have a trance or a divine encounter. Those are things you can desire, but they are not things that you can force to happen.

Instead, your assignment will be to set aside twenty minutes to be alone with God. Turn off your phone, computer, and all other distractions. In fact, for this exercise, I would even recommend that you not have music playing. Go to a place that is away from distracting noises and responsibilities.

Once there, ask the Holy Spirit to make you aware of God's presence with you. Wait in eager expectation for Him to reveal Himself in whatever way He chooses. Until you have some sort of awareness of His presence—whether it's subtle or profound—simply wait in silence. But once you have an awareness of Him, ask Him what He would like to do during your time together. Join Him in it.

If there's still time after you do that together, tell Him something you'd like to do. Perhaps sing to Him or tell Him about your struggles. Maybe draw a picture that expresses your heart, or perhaps ask Him questions.

When finished, find a notebook and journal about your experience.

SECTION 3:
Positioning Yourself for Revelation

DAY 11
ENCOUNTERING GOD IN THE SCRIPTURES

James Loruss

I do not think that a person who is not studying the Scriptures and who is not in the Word of God can honestly say that they are interested in the voice of God. You can't say, "I'm seeking God's will, and I'm listening to hear God's voice," if you're not reading the Scriptures because that is the basis, and that is what God has already revealed to us.... It all begins with the Word of God.

~ *Daniel Kolenda*

> **Luke 24:45** — Then [Jesus] opened their minds so they could understand the Scriptures. (NIV)

I USED TO HAVE A REALLY HARD TIME READING THE Bible. To put it bluntly, I really didn't enjoy reading the Bible at all. The first book I read all the way through was Revelation. "Why would you start there?" A great question I'd love to ask my 10 year old self. *Ah…that sounds like a good bedtime story; nothing like reading about a beast coming up out of the sea before I try to fall asleep.* Needless to say, reading the Bible just wasn't my favorite.

I felt this way for some time, until I heard this quote from Billy Graham: "The Bible is God's 'love letter' to us, telling us not only that He loves us, but showing us what He has done to demonstrate His love. It also tells us how we should live, because God knows what is best for us and He wants us to experience it."[1]

Suddenly, it was no longer a chore or an item to check off on my Christian to-do list. Reading the Bible became a journey of discovering the One I loved — the One who loved me first.

The way I read the Bible now is totally different. Did you know you can ask God questions about His book? He's just waiting for you to ask Him. Reading the Bible is supposed to be an experience with God. Bill Johnson has said, "Bible study without Bible experience is pointless."[2] It's not a quest for more knowledge but a quest to discover a Person.

It breaks my heart when I see people who can quote Scripture backwards and forwards yet don't carry the heart of God in their daily lives. Don't think it's possible? Look at the apostle Paul prior to his conversion. "Circumcised on the eighth day, of the people of Israel, of the tribe of Benjamin, a Hebrew of Hebrews; in regard to the law, a Pharisee; as for zeal, persecuting the church; as for righteousness based on the law, faultless" (Philippians 3:5-6). Paul knew the Scriptures and "in the name of God" slaughtered Christians. Paul thought he was doing right and justified his actions with Scripture. It's not enough to simply read and learn about the Bible—that much is clear. We need an encounter with the Almighty.

If we read the Bible the right way, we'll actually commune with God, and that's where our hearts and lives are transformed. Don't approach the text as just another book. See it as a love letter—a place to interact with the divine Author who inspired the hearts and minds of its human writers. Ask God questions as you read. Write down in a journal the things He makes known to you as you study. Take time to worship Him whenever He shows you something. Ask Him what He wants you to do with what you learned.

Ultimately, the Bible is the story of Jesus. And since our old, independent lives are dead and now Christ lives in us (Galatians 2:20), it is also a book that defines who we have been transformed into. God's desire is that you would peer into Scripture, encounter Him, and then see yourself the way you were created to be: like Jesus. (See James 1:22-24; 1 John 2:6; and 4:17.) He wants to spend time with you through His word. He has so much to say—so much to reveal to you. He desires to meet with you and teach you.

Just like Jesus opened the minds of His disciples to understand the Scriptures (Luke 24:45), pray that He would open your mind to understand and encounter Him in those sacred pages today.

Prayer Starter:

- ❑ Thank God for revealing His love so clearly to you through His Word.
- ❑ Ask God for an encounter with His presence in His written Scriptures.
- ❑ Ask God to show you which Scriptures to read that will best help you share His love with someone today.

Journal Experience:

Grab a Bible. Right now, ask the Holy Spirit if there is a specific topic He wants to speak to you about through the Bible today. If a topic comes to mind, write it down here:

_____

Whether or not anything came to mind, ask Jesus to open your mind to understand the Scriptures.

Now grab your Bible and read the 12th chapter of Romans. As you read, write down any realizations you have about the text. First write the verse number and then the thoughts you had about that verse.

_____
_____
_____
_____

_____

_____

_____

_____

_____

_____

_____

_____

_____

_____

_____

_____

_____

_____

_____

_____

_____

_____

_____

When you're finished, see if anything you wrote above applies to the topic the Holy Spirit said He wanted to speak to you about. If so, put a star by it above. If not, ask Him what book of the Bible He wants to speak to you in, and take some time to read the chapter(s) you feel led to. Keep reading until something strikes you that is in line with what He said He wanted to speak to you.

Action Step:

Ask the Holy Spirit to bring to your mind someone you know who could use some encouragement today.

Next, ask Him to remind you of a scripture verse that will be encouraging to this person.

If you don't know the reference, type what you know of the verse into Google.com and see if it provides a reference for you.

Write out the scripture with the reference (either handwritten in a note or in an e-mail or Facebook message), and then give it to the person you felt it was for. Let them know that you were praying for them, this scripture came to mind, and you felt it would be encouraging to them.

Supplemental Reading:
❏   Psalm 119:1-11

References:
1 Graham, Dr. Billy. "Billy Graham: Bible Is God's 'Love Letter' to Us." *Seattlepi.com*, Hearst Seattle Media, 6 Sept. 2007, 10:00pm, www.seattlepi.com/news/article/Billy-Graham-Bible-is-God-s-love-letter-to-us-1246557.php.
2 Johnson, Bill. "Bethel Church, Redding." *Bethel Church, Redding, Facebook Posts,* Facebook, 26 Aug. 2010, 10:33am, www.facebook.com/bethel.church.redding/posts/1456 75912130102.

DAY 12
LOVING WHAT GOD LOVES

Art Thomas

What I came to understand is if you have God's heart, you know what God knows.

~ Loren Sandford

> **John 3:16-17** — For God so loved the world that He gave His one and only Son, that whoever believes in Him shall not perish but have eternal life. For God did not send His Son into the world to condemn the world, but to save the world through Him. (NIV)

THE MORE IN-TUNE WE BECOME WITH THE HEART OF God, the more easily we can recognize how He feels about different people and their circumstances. And when we know how He feels, it's much easier to discern what He's saying.

On the other side of the coin, if we love the

things God hates, then our hearing becomes muddled as we struggle to reconcile what we enjoy with what God is actually saying.

First John 2:15-16 says, "Do not love the world or anything in the world. If anyone loves the world, love for the Father is not in them. For everything in the world — the lust of the flesh, the lust of the eyes, and the pride of life — comes not from the Father but from the world." This may seem to contradict John 3:16, which says that God loves the world, but that passage is about the people of the world whereas this verse is about the systems and ways of the world (not the people).

In other words, one of the most effective ways to unite yourself with the heart of God is to disregard such worthless, worldly things as lust and pride (serving yourself) and then engage in actively loving the people all around you (serving them).

Love is heartfelt service. Love is self-sacrifice. If you're sacrificing your time, money, energy, and/or talents to satisfy your own lusts, indulge your greed, or boost your ego, then you are completely disengaged from the love of God. Accordingly, you'll find yourself listening for Him to talk about the things you care about (namely your own interests) and ignoring Him when He challenges your current condition. The ultimate end of such a focus is that you may begin to listen to whatever spirit will tell you what you want to hear. The natural outcome is deception.

But if you willingly self-sacrifice your time, money, energy, and/or talents in selfless service to others (fueled by passion for Jesus), then you are indeed partnering with the heart of God. In this case you'll find yourself listening for Him to speak about things that will aid and empower you to love others more effectively, and you'll be sensitive to His correction in your life.

The Father sent Jesus as an active expression of His love—self-sacrificing for the sake of a humanity who didn't deserve it. Romans 5:8 says, "But God demonstrates His own love for us in this: While we were still sinners, Christ died for us."

In Philippians 1:9-10, Paul prays that our "love may abound...so that you may be able to discern what is best..." Love sharpens discernment. If you want to receive clearer revelation from the Lord, learn to love what He loves (or, rather, *who* He loves), and distance yourself from everything He hates.

Proverbs 6:17-19 tells us exactly what God hates: "haughty eyes, a lying tongue, hands that shed innocent blood, a heart that devises wicked schemes, feet that are quick to rush into evil, a false witness who pours out lies, and a person who stirs up conflict in the community." In summary, God hates anything and everything in this world that brings confusion, pain, death, and heartache to the multitudes of people He loves so dearly. John 3:16 and Romans 5:8 tell us clearly who He loves: the whole world—both saints and sinners.

Learn to personally sacrifice for the things— rather, the *people*—for whom God sacrificed through Jesus, and you'll quickly become an active expression of His heart to the world.

Prayer Starter:

- ❑ Thank God for loving you first when you least deserved it.
- ❑ Ask the Holy Spirit to show you any area of your life where you have loved the things of the world—the lust of the flesh, the lust of the eyes, and the pride of life.
- ❑ Ask the Holy Spirit to help you see people the way God sees them and to help you effectively express His love to them.

Journal Experience:

Think of the person who bothers you, frustrates you, or annoys you the most (or the most frequently). Ask Jesus to tell you what He thinks of that person. Write down the thoughts that come to mind.

_____

_____

_____

_____

_____

_____

_____

_____

_____

_____

_____

_____

_____

_____

_____

_____

_____

_____

_____

_____

_____

_____

_____

_____

Action Step:

Write a note (or an e-mail or Facebook message) to the person you thought of during the Journal Experience. Start with something like, "I was praying for you, and I felt like God showed me some of His thoughts about you. Here's what I feel He said…"

If that person is also doing this study, I recommend being wise about this exercise. If they are fully aware that there is an emotional rift between you both, this could be an incredibly healing exercise. But if they aren't aware — perhaps you're simply annoyed by a personality quirk or emotional deficiency — discovering through this exercise that they annoy you could be relationally damaging (the opposite of what we're going for). Only send the note if the person will not connect it to this assignment.

Supplemental Reading:
❑ Romans 12:9-10

DAY 13
SUBMISSION TO JESUS AS LORD

Jonathan Ammon

Obedience is an act of love. It's an act of trust. My obedience is to say to God, "I know Your is heart for me. And I know that if I do what You tell me to do, it will be good for me and for others because You love me."

~ *R. Loren Sandford*

> **John 8:47** — Whoever belongs to God hears what God says. The reason you do not hear is that you do not belong to God. (NIV)

ONE OF THE GREAT TENSIONS AND PARADOXES IN Scripture is that in Jesus' teachings and parables He refers to us as both sons and servants. In both cases we belong to God. We are owned by Him—created by Him and for Him. Our lives are not our own, and we exist to glorify God through a love relationship with Him. Both servants and children must obey the authority over them.

Jesus is our Friend, our Brother, and our Master. He is the King of kings and the Lord of lords, the Head of all authority, and the Source of our authority as believers in Christ. In order to have a right relationship with Jesus or relate to Jesus in the correct way, we must relate to Him as our Lord and Master — as the absolute authority in our lives. When we hear God's voice, we hear the voice of Love and the voice of our Master who deserves absolute submission to His command.

Those who have submitted to Christ as Lord and Master have positioned themselves to hear His voice because they are prepared to respond to whatever He says. "Whoever belongs to God hears what God says." In the rebellion of our flesh, we often resist the voice and command of the Lord. Either we hear and do not obey, or we harden our hearts and stop listening because we fear our Master's command (rather than trusting His love and leadership). Many of the stories in this book and its accompanying film episodes are stories where God instructed someone in what to do. In order to have these testimonies, we must obey. As we grow in obedience and submission, God will give us greater and greater tasks, and we will glorify Him more and more.

Near the end of His earthly life, Jesus told His disciples, "There is so much more I want to tell you, but you can't bear it now" (John 16:2). There are so many things that God desires to tell us. He waits on our maturity and our obedience. As we grow in Him — in complete abandonment to His love, will, and leadership — we receive more from His heart and mind. We hear the voice of the Master, and we don't turn away. We hear it as the voice of Love leading us into all the joy of His presence and the knowledge of Christ.

Prayer Starter:

- ❑ Praise and Worship Jesus as Lord and Master. Re-vocalize your decision of surrender to Jesus and your desire to remain completely dedicated to Him.
- ❑ Ask the Lord to reveal any rebellion in your heart. Offer these things to God. Repent and ask God to reveal His love and trustworthiness in that specific area.
- ❑ Ask God to assert His authority in your daily life and relationships. Give Him permission to interrupt you with orders and commands for your day. Do your best to listen and follow through on anything you sense God telling you.

Journal Experience:

Ask God if there is any area of your life or heart where you haven't trusted Him as Master. Ask Him if there is any area — big or small — that you have walled off from His touch or that you have not yet fully surrendered to Him. Write down what comes to mind.

_____

_____

_____

_____

_____

_____

_____

_____

Ask God to identify the original source of that area of rebellion, fear, or independence. Was it a specific traumatic event? Ongoing issues throughout childhood? Recent or present influences in your life? Ask God if there is a lie you've believed that has caused this in your heart.

_____

_____

_____

_____

_____

_____

_____

_____

_____

_____

_____

_____

_____

_____

_____

_____

_____

_____

Ask God if there is something He wants you to do to submit to Him in that area of your life.

_____

_____

_____

_____

_____

_____

_____

Ask God if there is something that He wants to tell you now that you've processed this experience. "Lord, is there something You want to tell me that You couldn't tell me before?"

_____

_____

_____

_____

_____

_____

_____

Action Step:

During the Journal Experience, you asked God if there was anything He wanted you to do to submit to Him in this area of your life. If He showed you something easy to accomplish, do it today. If He showed you something bigger or more difficult to do, identify the first steps toward that end, and put the plan into motion.

And if God did not show you anything specific to do, then at least share with someone the testimony of what you just processed with the Lord. Tell them about the lie you believed, the truth God revealed to you, and the difference it made in your heart.

Supplemental Reading:
❑ Luke 6:46-49

DAY 14
LISTENING TO OTHERS

Jonathan Ammon

God made a family, and He loves when we can love each other... I've seen a lot of times where He'll hide my breakthrough in someone else because He's teaching me not independence but interdependence — that we would be one as the Body of Christ.

~ *Lacey Thompson*

> **Acts 2:17-18** — In the last days, God says, I will pour out My Spirit on all people. Your sons and daughters will prophesy, your young men will see visions, your old men will dream dreams. Even on My servants, both men and women, I will pour out My Spirit in those days, and they will prophesy. (NIV)

WHEN GOD POURED OUT HIS SPIRIT ON THE DAY OF Pentecost, He birthed the Church—a prophetic community. Every single believer received the

Spirit's enablement and permission to prophesy. God created a new priesthood that included every single believer.

Romans 8:14 identifies every child of God as someone who is led by God's Spirit: "For as many as are led by the Spirit of God, these are sons of God." If you are a child of God, you are a prophetically-led individual, and so is the believer next to you. So is the Christian community around you. "So then, my beloved brethren, let every man be swift to hear, slow to speak..." (James 1:19, NKJV).

In the Old Covenant (before Jesus), the Holy Spirit empowered only a few individuals who were called to lead the people of God. Today the entire believing community is saturated with the Spirit of God. The entire community has access to God's voice and leading. The entire community has access to the Spirit's discernment and guidance. If we want to hear God, we must honor His voice in His Church.

If we want to claim for ourselves God's promises of prophecy for every believer, we must acknowledge those promises for the people around us. If we really believe those promises, we must believe that God has the ability to speak to us through any one of our brothers and sisters around us. We must honor God's work in their lives, and we must not turn a deaf ear to what God may be saying through the person next to us. When people who have the mind of Christ speak, it is natural for God's thoughts to be proclaimed — and often we do so without realizing it.

I can't relate how many times I have been struck, convicted, encouraged, and challenged in a deeply personal way when listening to another believer share a testimony, something they've been learning, or a prophetic word. Sometimes these words come from what I would consider the most unlikely places. But I know that it is God's desire to speak through every believer. I know that He does. And so I listen.

God no longer desires a single prophet leading His people. He desires a prophetic community functioning in love, testing and weighing what is said, guarding and guiding one another. I have misheard God many times, but when I have taken to others what I mistakenly felt God was saying, the community of faith has corrected me and helped me grow in hearing God. We are all meant to hear God through one another.

If you aren't good at listening to others, you might not be good at listening at all. You might not be good at listening to God's Spirit. Hearing God's voice means recognizing it in all the small, familiar places. That includes recognizing Christ's Church — His body.

If you take what God says through others in common settings seriously, He will use those things to transform your life. "Whoever can be trusted with very little can also be trusted with much..." (Luke 16:10). Recognizing God's voice — even in simple conversation with others — will lead to greater revelation in other areas of our lives.

Prayer Starter:

- ❑ Thank God that He speaks through His people. Ask God to speak to you through others this week. Ask God for specific confirmations and instructions in your conversations with others.
- ❑ Ask God to give you a humble and teachable heart that is eager to learn from others. Ask God to help you believe in His voice through other people and to help you honor others above yourself.
- ❑ Pray that your conversation would be salted with God's Word and message and that you would unknowingly speak from God's heart in everyday conversation.

Journal Experience:

Ask God if there are any obstacles in your heart to trusting others and listening well. Write down what comes to mind.

_____

_____

_____

_____

_____

_____

_____

_____

_____

_____

_____

Ask God to touch those areas of your heart and show you what needs to be surrendered or addressed in your own heart. Is there anyone you need to forgive? Write down what you feel or experience during this time of meeting with the Lord.

_____

_____

_____

_____

_____

_____

_____

_____

_____

_____

_____

_____

_____

_____

_____

_____

_____

_____

_____

Action Step:

Listen carefully to other believers when in conversation or community today (or anytime this week). If you don't expect to have a natural opportunity for such interaction, simply contact a fellow believer and ask him or her what God has been teaching them most recently. Listen intently.

Identify and write down at least one thing that God made personal to you in what another believer said.

Encourage that person that you heard God through them.

_____

_____

_____

_____

_____

Supplemental Reading:
❑   1 Corinthians 14
❑   2 Chronicles 20

DAY 15
STEWARDING EARLIER REVELATION

Art Thomas

There's a principle — it's not my idea, it's Jesus' idea — that 'he who is faithful in little will be made ruler over much.' If you're not faithful to steward the words that God has given us… then you are never going to be the person that God begins to reveal deep mysteries to on a one-on-one basis.

~ Daniel Kolenda

> **1 Corinthians 4:1-2** — This, then, is how you ought to regard us: as servants of Christ and as those entrusted with the mysteries God has revealed. Now it is required that those who have been given a trust must prove faithful. (NIV)

GOD LOVES TO REVEAL TRUTH TO HIS CHILDREN. Every nugget of truth that He reveals is an encounter with Jesus because Jesus is the bodily expression of truth. (See John 14:6 and Hebrews 1:3.)

As with any blessing from God, revelation is given by grace—not because we deserve it but simply because He loves us. However, there is a powerful principle that affects future blessings, and that is how faithfully we steward today's blessings.

In Matthew 25:14-30, Jesus tells a parable about the kingdom of heaven that teaches us the importance of good stewardship. In the story, a rich man goes on a journey and leaves a different amount of gold with three different servants. To the first servant, he gave five bags of gold, to the second two, and to the third, one.

Verse 15 says that he distributed the gold according to each worker's ability. I used to feel bad for the third servant who only received one bag of gold. I thought it was unfair that the master only gave him one bag and still expected a return on his money. But each bag of gold was worth about twenty years of wages for the typical day-worker of the time! Even this servant who wasn't trustworthy received a substantial sum of money to work with.

Like the rich man did for his servants, God distributes revelation to us according to our ability— by this I am referring to our track record of handling that revelation well in the past. When people treasure intimacy with God and partner with Him to share revelation in healthy ways that help others grow and encounter the love of God, He loves to give them greater responsibility with weightier revelation.

Sometimes we look at certain ministers and wish we could preach or teach with the level of wisdom and revelation in which they walk. But we miss the fact that their ministries are simply demonstrations of a lifetime of stewarding revelation well and God responding with greater revelation. Never compare or judge the value of something God reveals to you. If you think that your own revelation is so small that it's insignificant to the Kingdom, you won't invest that revelation into the lives of others. But the reality is that even the smallest revelation is more valuable than anything you could have come up with on your own. Even one bag of gold was worth twenty years of wages.

In today's scripture passage, the "mysteries" Paul was talking about referred specifically to the Gospel. The Good News about Jesus is the first revelation given to every single believer. How you steward the Good News that has been entrusted to you will have a direct affect on what sort of revelation you're able to walk in.

Anyone who wants to have deep revelation about the things of God needs to faithfully share the simple Gospel whenever they have the opportunity. God will honor you for your faithfulness and entrust more to you. As the rich man said to the two servants who stewarded their gold well, "You have been faithful with a few things; I will put you in charge of many things" (Matthew 25:21, 23).

In practical terms, good stewardship of revelation begins with writing down what God shows you. In Habakkuk 2:2, God instructed the prophet, "Write down the revelation and make it plain on tablets so that a herald may run with it." When we write down what God has spoken to us, we leave no room for the enemy to question us as he did the woman in the garden: "Did God really say...?" When Jesus was tempted in the wilderness, He answered, "It is written..." There is significant value in writing down what God has spoken.

Once you've written down what the Lord has shown you, ask Him what to do with it. Should it be shared with a particular person? Do you have a voice in a particular group of people to share it with? Should you study further to understand it better? Should you write an article or a book about it? Should you do something creative with it, like write a song? Do whatever the Lord puts on your heart, and you will be faithfully stewarding the revelation God gave you.

And above all, love people with the things God shows you. Paul said that "knowledge puffs up while love builds up" (1 Corinthians 8:1). Every time I learn something new, my next prayer is, "Lord, teach me to love with what You just showed me." Sometimes the most loving thing you can do with what you know is to not share it. Sometimes good stewardship involves waiting until the right moment to share with the right audience. I used to have a bad habit (and sometimes still struggle) that every time someone shared with me something God taught them, I would want to reply with everything God has shown me about that same topic. I thought I was helping, but it usually translated to people as though their revelation was inferior and I was trying to one-up them. Love values others. As Paul also said, "If I have the gift of prophecy and can fathom all mysteries and all knowledge... but do not have love, I am nothing" (1 Corinthians 13:2).

Honor God with the level of revelation you've received—even if it's nothing more than the simple Gospel revealed in the Bible. Even so-called "small" revelation is highly valuable. If you're faithful with it, God will show you more.

Prayer Starter:

- ❏ Thank God for revealing things to you in the Bible. Ask Him to reveal more to you.
- ❏ Ask the Holy Spirit to help you faithfully steward the level of revelation you've received.
- ❏ Ask God to help you better understand the Gospel so that you can share it more effectively with people.

Journal Experience:

Write down the latest thing God revealed to you about Himself or your relationship with Him. Perhaps it's something you realized while reading this book, praying, listening to a sermon, or studying Scripture.

Alternatively, write down something you know God has spoken to you in the past that you either haven't acted on yet or have been deliberately procrastinating on.

If you can't think of anything, write a summary of your current understanding of the Good News. What did Jesus purchase with His blood? What is available to us because of Jesus' sacrifice? What do human beings have to do in order to experience and receive this Gospel?

Keep your answer simple enough to fit in the limited space but descriptive enough that someone reading it could be led to Jesus through your words.

_____

_____

_____

_____

_____

_____

_____

_____

_____

_____

_____

_____

_____

_____

_____

Action Step:

Ask the Lord what He wants you to do with what you wrote down in the Journal Experience. Today, either do what He tells you or do a first step or two toward what He tells you. If you're not sure what the first step is, ask Him.

Supplemental Reading:
❏ Matthew 25:14-30

SECTION 4:
How to Judge Revelation

DAY 16
DOES IT LINE UP WITH SCRIPTURE?

Art Thomas

The Scriptures are a window into the heart of God. In fact, they are the heart of God on paper.

~ *Michael Koulianos*

> **2 Timothy 3:16-17** — All Scripture is God-breathed and is useful for teaching, rebuking, correcting and training in righteousness, so that the servant of God may be thoroughly equipped for every good work. (NIV)

THE BIBLE GIVES US CLEAR INSIGHT INTO THE HEART and mind of God. From cover to cover, it is the story of Jesus—why He needed to come, how and when He came, what He taught and did, what He continues to do, and what He plans for the future.

Throughout the centuries, this text has been proven true time and again with countless

119

prophecies having been fulfilled. For this reason Peter calls the Scriptures "the prophetic word made more sure" (2 Peter 1:19, NASB). When you read the Bible, you can let down your guard and wholeheartedly accept it as God's word to man.

Not so with other forms of prophecy. Too much room for error exists in the fact that "we know in part and we prophesy in part" (1 Corinthians 13:9). No one has the full picture of everything God is saying. When we hear typical prophetic words, we need to engage in discernment (1 Corinthians 14:29). But when we read the Bible, there is no need to discern. The discerning has already been done by the proof of history — prayerfully debated in Church councils and found to be truth through unfolding archaeology, reason, and the personal experience of millions of people.

Perhaps you've heard of the "canonization" of Scripture. During the first few centuries of the Church, there were so many letters and "gospels" floating around (all claiming to be true) that the early Church fathers decided there needed to be some sort of standard that they could support as valid Scripture. I admit that I am oversimplifying the history behind the "canon" you use in your Bible today, but simply know that much thought, debate, study, experience, prayer, and dedication went into its development.

The word "canon" comes from a Greek word that means "measuring rod." You could say that the idea behind the Canon is that it would become the "measuring rod" against which we test all other revelation. If what someone claims they heard from God disagrees with the "prophetic word made more sure," then it doesn't measure up and must be discarded.

Biblical knowledge isn't necessary in order to prophesy, but it does enable you to discern "on the fly" as prophecies are being spoken. This is one of the reasons Biblical study is valuable and worth the investment of your time and attention.

I remember when I first started experiencing visions. One of the first things the Lord showed me was an ocean of angels, as far as the eye could see. I remembered in that moment about what John saw in Revelation: "...many angels, numbering thousands upon thousands, and ten thousand times ten thousand. They encircled the throne..." (See Revelation 5:11.) I knew, based on biblical knowledge, that this was a valid vision.

I said, "Jesus, I don't want to be with the angels. I want to be with You!"

At that moment I sensed Him right next to me, and in the vision (not my physical ears), He whispered to me, "You *are* with Me. Your place is not out there, lost in the ocean of angels. Your place is to sit here with Me on My throne."

I immediately snapped out of the vision. What I thought I heard seemed prideful—perhaps even heretical. I knew the first part—the ocean of angels—lined up with Scripture, but I felt uncomfortable about the second part.

I wrote down what I saw and admitted that it made me uncomfortable. Then I started to read the book of Revelation for clues (since that's where I knew the first part was found). It wasn't long before I came across Revelation 3:21, in which Jesus says, "To the one who is victorious, I will give the right to sit with Me on My throne, just as I was victorious and sat down with My Father on His throne."

A quick look at the cross-reference in my Bible's margin took me to Ephesians 2:6, which says, "And God raised us up with Christ and seated us with Him in the heavenly realms in Christ Jesus."

It was true! I suddenly knew I'd had a true vision from the Lord. "The prophetic word made more sure" confirmed the vision I had in my mind, and I then knew I had heard from the Lord.

This teaching about being seated on the throne with Christ has become part of the heartbeat of my ministry. The vision God gave me awakened me to a reality I had not previously seen, and the Scriptures proved it true.

Prayer Starter:

❑ Thank God for preserving the Scriptures through the millennia and for making them so easily available to you today.
❑ Ask God to open the eyes of your heart to understand the Scriptures more fully.
❑ Ask the Lord to either alert you to people in your life who can instruct you in studying the Scriptures or to bring new people into your life to do the same.

Special Note:
If you're unfamiliar with looking up verses, your Bible should have a Table of Contents in the front that will help you find the page number for each book. The big numbers that separate sections in each book are the "chapter numbers," and the little numbers that flow in the text are "verse numbers." For example: in "Revelation 3:21," "Revelation" is the name of the book; "3" is the chapter number; and "21" is the verse number.

Journal Experience:

Ask the Lord, "What do You think of me?" Write down what comes to your mind.

_____

_____

_____

_____

_____

_____

_____

_____

_____

_____

_____

_____

_____

_____

_____

_____

_____

_____

_____

_____

_____

_____

_____

_____

Now, grab a Bible and look up the following four Scripture passages:

➔ *1 John 4:15-19*   ➔ *Romans 8:35-39*
➔ *2 Corinthians 5:17-21*   ➔ *1 Peter 2:9*

Is what you wrote consistent with what you see in these scriptures? Don't focus so much on whether or not things line up perfectly. But as broad, sweeping principles: Do the things you wrote and the things you read sound like they came from the same divine Inspirer? Is what you wrote consistent with the love of God and with your transformed identity in Christ?

Place a star next to each thing you wrote that lines up. Place a question mark next to each thing you're not sure about. And if see something is completely incorrect, strike a line through it.

Action Step:

Take time to memorize 2 Timothy 3:16-17 (note that this is the scripture written on page 119 at the beginning of this lesson). When you've got it, ask someone to check you on it while you recite it.

Supplemental Reading:
❑   Romans 15:4
❑   2 Peter 1:16-21

DAY 17
DOES IT SOUND AND FEEL LIKE JESUS

James Loruss

---

*God's voice sounds like God's nature and God's character.
We know that His voice always sounds like love because
He is love. It's kind; it's gracious; it's filled with power.*
~ Jonathan Ammon

> **John 10:2-5** — The one who enters by the
> gate is the shepherd of the sheep. The
> gatekeeper opens the gate for him, and
> the sheep listen to his voice. He calls his
> own sheep by name and leads them out.
> When he has brought out all his own, he
> goes on ahead of them, and his sheep
> follow him because they know his voice.
> But they will never follow a stranger; in
> fact, they will run away from him because
> they do not recognize a stranger's voice."
> (NIV)

GOD'S VOICE IS DISTINCT. I FIND THE MORE THAT I

get to know Him as a Person, the more effectively I can hear His voice. We can't separate the person of God from the voice of God.

Knowing who you're listening to is important. Spending time with Jesus in the quiet place when it's just you and Him is essential to hearing His voice in the busyness of everyday life.

I remember being at my Dad's birthday party when I was younger and hearing my mom from across the room tell some story mentioning my name. Suddenly my ears perked up. Everything else in that moment stopped because I was now fixed on my mom's voice—probably because I wanted to hear what she was saying about me. I remember the Lord years later reminding me of this memory to teach me a lesson. He showed me that the reason I was so attentive to my mom's voice was because I had spent time learning what it sounded like.

Maybe this is a bit odd, but have you ever noticed you can identify your close friends even by the sound of their cough? Sounds crazy, but I bet you'd be surprised how well you can recognize someone by something so simple.

The reason you can recognize someone's voice, sound, smell, silhouette, or even pace of footsteps is because you've become familiar with that person through time. The same goes for how we identify God's voice.

I saw a calendar once that presented a different scripture verse each day. One day it listed Matthew 4:9, which says, "'All this I will give you,' he said, 'if you will bow down and worship me.'" That sounded encouraging, but it didn't sit right with me. Then I read in context and saw it was Satan who said it! (Someone didn't do their homework.)

Second Corinthians 11:14 says that "Satan masquerades as an angel of light." So how can we ever be sure who we're listening to? The key is intimacy. When you spend quality time with Jesus, you grow in your ability to discern His voice. Getting to know Him and getting to know His voice are the same; they can't be separated. The "secret" to knowing the voice of God is intimacy and time spent together.

Consider again today's opening scripture: "...and his sheep follow him because they know his voice. But they will never follow a stranger; in fact, they will run away from him because they do not recognize a stranger's voice." Learning to recognize how God's voice sounds and the way it feels comes through intimacy. I like how one minister, Dan Mohler, says it: "A stranger's voice sounds strange." God's voice will not always be comfortable, but it will be familiar to His children. I don't think it's coincidence that the most "at home" feeling we can have is in God's presence.

Our assurance is found in knowing Him. If you've accepted Jesus as Lord, that means you know His voice. John 6:44-45 tells us that no one comes to Jesus unless the Father first draws them. The fact that you are following God is proof that you have already recognized His voice. You already know your Shepherd. If you never trust God to speak to you through His indwelling Spirit, you'll always excuse away His voice. Trust His voice whenever it sounds and feels like the Jesus you know. And take the time to know Him more intimately so that His voice is easier and easier to recognize.

If you're questioning whether or not you're hearing His voice today, start with studying Jesus.

Study His life. First read the Gospel accounts of Matthew, Mark, Luke, and John to be sure you're truly familiar with Him (I recommend starting with Mark).

If what you hear contradicts the Bible, scrap it. But some things aren't expressly stated in the Bible. The Bible may tell you how to have a good marriage, but it doesn't tell you who to marry or when. For these things, the next test is to ask whether what we're hearing sounds and feels like Jesus.

So study the Bible first. But more importantly, go beyond reading and on to experience. Choose to engage Him as a Person and not just a historical figure. Like any relationship, your familiarity with Him will grow with quality time spent together. Meet with Him in the place of silence and prayer. He's waiting to encounter you.

Prayer Starter:

- ❑ Thank God for being trustworthy.
- ❑ Ask the Holy Spirit if there's any area of your life that's contradicting God's character or the way that Jesus lived.
- ❑ Ask God to give you an opportunity to share the Gospel with someone today.

Journal Experience:

Find a timer (perhaps on your phone) and set it for 3-5 minutes (a timer is better than a clock because it will allow you to focus on what you're doing and not keep looking at the clock). During this time, remain completely silent before the Lord. Choose to recognize His presence in the room with you right now. Write down your reflections on the experience. Did He say anything to you? What did you feel or sense during this time?

_____

_____

_____

_____

_____

_____

_____

_____

_____

_____

_____

_____

_____

_____

_____

_____

_____

_____

_____

_____

_____

_____

_____

_____

_____

_____

_____

Action Step:

Not all of our encounters with the Lord are meant to be shared with others. Ask the Lord if you can tell someone else about your most recent encounter with Him (like today's Journal Experience). If He says "yes," ask Him who would be encouraged today by it. If He says "no," ask Him what He does want you to say and to whom — then share that.

Supplemental Reading:
- ❑ Psalm 46
- ❑ Matthew 6:6-8

DAY 18
EXAMINING THE DESIRES OF YOUR HEART

Jonathan Ammon (with Art Thomas)

You have to get beyond your own emotions. Another rule of prophetic ministry is that human emotion is a lens that distorts the voice of God. I have to get past what I feel. What does the Father feel? Where is the peace and the heart of God? If I can get there, then I have a sense of what's going on.

~ R. Loren Sandford

> 2 Timothy 4:3-4 — For the time will come when people will not put up with sound doctrine. Instead, to suit their own desires, they will gather around them a great number of teachers to say what their itching ears want to hear. They will turn their ears away from the truth and turn aside to myths. (NIV)

WE DON'T KNOW WHAT'S BEST FOR OURSELVES. WE

don't have the ability to see all the consequences of our actions, the chain reactions of our decisions, or the future that God intends for us. We are not meant to be able to figure things out on our own. We were meant to follow a Shepherd and obey a Master. We were designed to receive guidance.

We have a loving Father who is perfect in knowledge and knows what is best for us in every situation. He works with our desires, and He gives us new ones. Often He works beyond our desires, challenging us to act out of selfless love.

In context, today's scripture applies to teachings spoken by others. But the principle behind it also has implications for God's words spoken directly to us. How often do we only listen for God to speak what we want Him to say and instead find ourselves deceived? How often do we search for any feeling or sign that will confirm our own desires and ignore anything to the contrary?

Sometimes the desires of our own hearts can cloud what we're hearing. Those desires can make us think we're hearing God when in truth we only hear the echo chamber of our own heart. Worse yet, we may open ourselves up to listen to any spirit who will tell us what we want to hear. The more intensely you desire something to happen, the harder it often is to know if you're hearing God.

When our heart is set on something, we often want God's permission to go after it. We want to hear God say, "Yes." We have a tendency to interpret small details as signs from God that we are to pursue our heart's desire.

Often friends who care for us are eager to confirm that "God wants you to follow your heart." Unfortunately, our hearts and desires are not perfect.

Even our desire for good things can sometimes miss God's best plan.

It is often easier to hear God's voice when His direction cuts across our desire. We instinctively and instantly know, "That did not originate from me because that is definitely not what I would choose or what I want to do right now." When we are honest about (1) who we are and (2) our desires and about (3) who God is and (4) what He desires, we begin to have reference points to discern what comes from our own hearts and what comes from God.

Small, impersonal "signs" that confirm our desires should be judged and tested well. We should ask for continued confirmation. Issues where our emotions run high—such as family and romance—should be approached with biblical wisdom, council, and input from others. We often have strong emotions when we hear God's voice, but the majority of the time our strong emotions are not the voice of God.

When judging revelation, first start with the test of Scripture. Does it contradict the Bible or does it seem to fit? Next ask if it sounds and feels like the Jesus you've come to know. Is it consistent with His heart and nature? After it passes the first two tests, do a heart-check. Is this something you were really hoping God would say? If so, it may still truly be Him; but proceed with caution. Ask others to help discern. Ask God for clearer confirmation. Take time.

In order to hear God clearly, we must lay our desires aside and sincerely pursue His. We must know and trust that His plans for us are better than we could hope or imagine and that regardless of what we want right now, His plan will fulfill the best desires of our hearts.

Prayer Starter:

- ❑ Thank God for His guidance and protection. Thank Him for the promise that as we delight in Him, He gives us the desires of our hearts.
- ❑ Ask God to purify your heart and give you His desires.
- ❑ Ask God to help you hear clearly and have a heart for His glory and a heart to bless others.

Journal Experience:

Write down a list of personal desires that you have for your life. Don't try to make it a holy list. Be extremely honest and transparent.

_____

_____

_____

_____

_____

_____

_____

_____

_____

_____

_____

_____

_____

Now write a list of specific things that you know God wants for your life. (If you're not sure, ask Him.)

_____

_____

_____

_____

_____

_____

_____

_____

_____

_____

_____

Are there any overlaps in the two lists? That's not a bad thing! Identify any areas where you may need to be careful in discerning God's voice and direction. What are some safeguards you can place on those things to help you discern more effectively?

_____

_____

_____

_____

_____

_____

_____

_____

_____

_____

Action Step:

Is there anything on the list of God's desires on the previous page that you don't like doing or aren't excited about? Is there anything that is difficult for you to do? Ask God to give you a specific, manageable task to help you grow in that area.

If He tells you something you can implement today, do it. If He tells you something you can only do later, tell a friend and ask them to keep you accountable.

You may want to take note of what He says:

_____

_____

_____

_____

Supplemental Reading:
❏ Jeremiah 23:9-40

DAY 19
WHAT DO OTHER BELIEVERS THINK?

James Loruss

All of us can be wrong... There is a community of faith that hears the voice of God together. And because that community of faith is more than one person, there is safety even if someone is wrong. But that safety only exists if we're willing to correct – if we're willing to acknowledge that we're wrong and willing to grow together in hearing the voice of God.

~ Jonathan Ammon

> **1 Corinthians 14:29** — Two or three prophets should speak, and the others should weigh carefully what is said. (NIV)

THE DAY THAT YOU SURRENDERED TO JESUS AS LORD of your life was the day you were adopted into the family of God. And whether you like it or not, they are your family for eternity. You are now a part of a family that crosses every social class, every national border, and even every difference of opinion. We are all one body.

Ephesians 4:3-6 says, "Make every effort to keep the unity of the Spirit through the bond of peace. There is one body and one Spirit, just as you were called to one hope when you were called; one Lord, one faith, one baptism; one God and Father of all, who is over all and through all and in all." In the same way that there is one God, there is only one body.

Jesus is not coming back for a dismembered Bride. We are called to unity. God is not in disunity with Himself, and neither should the Body of Christ. If you have a disagreement with a blood relative, does your disagreement make them no longer related to you? Does your blood suddenly become different from theirs? No! The blood of Jesus was shed for you, but it was also shed for your brothers and sisters in Christ. They are just as redeemed as you are, even if they disagree with you.

God's check-and-balance system for hearing His voice is a family. He wants to drive us into community with one another. First Corinthians 14:29 teaches us to discern what other people speak prophetically. God keeps us in community for our own good. It's easy to hear and believe crazy things when you have no one in your life who loves you enough to question what you say.

I'm always a bit leery when someone who is not actively engaging in a Christian community wants to give me a prophetic word. I've seen people who I love and care for start out in community and then gradually begin to drift into isolation. That's when they get into weird stuff. They begin to hear their own desires instead of Jesus' desires and those of His Body.

Speaking on God's behalf apart from the context of Christian community is selfish, and our God is not selfish. God puts us in community to keep us grounded in love. It's hard to remain selfish for a long time when you're active in a healthy community of believers.

First Corinthians 13:2 warns, "If I have the gift of prophecy and can fathom all mysteries and all knowledge...but do not have love, I am nothing." We must remain in love if we want to stay healthy. It's a lot easier to *think* you're hearing God's voice 100% of the time when you don't let anyone correct you. It's easier, but it's unhealthy and incredibly dangerous.

In First Corinthians 11:29 — two chapters before this warning about love — Paul addresses the Corinthian church about their failure to discern the body of Christ. He corrects them for the divisions, disunity, and exclusive cliques among them. Their lack of love and their inability to see the value in each other brought them under judgment from God.

I believe that the more we choose to see the Spirit of Christ dwelling in every believer, the better we'll hear His voice. We need to love and care for one another and honor God by honoring His Spirit inside them. It is impossible to respect and honor Jesus' voice when you don't respect and honor His body. We must remain in community. Jesus' physical body was broken so His body (the Church) can be whole.

When judging revelation, first check with Scripture. Then check it against the nature of Jesus. Examine your own desires and take any necessary precautions. Finally, run it by other believers —

including the ones who you "know" will disagree with you. They may bring up valid points that would not have been discovered if you had only checked with people who you expect to agree with you. We are all a family, and we need each other.

Prayer Starter:

- ❑ Thank God that He has brought you into a family. Thank Him for your brothers and sisters in Christ.
- ❑ Ask the Holy Spirit if there is any bitterness in your heart toward other believers.
- ❑ Pray for other believers by name—people you know. Pray that the church would be unified through Christ and Christ alone.

Journal Experience:

Ask the Holy Spirit if you've been avoiding Christian community (either avoiding it altogether or avoiding fully engaging in it in some way). If the answer is yes, Ask the Lord why. Were you hurt by a brother or sister in Christ? Are you afraid to open up for some reason? Write a letter to Jesus. Ask Him to cleanse you of any bitterness, and choose to forgive any people who may have wronged you. Ask Him to help you develop deeper and truer relationships.

_____

_____

_____

_____

_____

_____

_____

_____

_____

_____

_____

_____

_____

_____

_____

_____

_____

Action Step:

If you have been avoiding community because of fear of vulnerability or past hurts, take a practical step today towards reconciliation. Contact someone who may have wronged you or who you've been avoiding. Ask for forgiveness for your part in the strained relationship. Pray that God would bless that person.

Supplemental Reading:
❑ John 17:20-26

DAY 20
DOES IT PRODUCE GOOD FRUIT?

Jonathan Ammon

A lot of people claim to have prophetic encounters. "This angel came down and spoke with me." But if your encounter does not lead to life-transformation, it's bogus.
~ *Rick Pino*

> **Psalm 119:130** — The unfolding of your words gives light; it gives understanding to the simple. (NIV)
>
> **Jeremiah 15:16** — When your words came, I ate them; they were my joy and my heart's delight, for I bear your name, Lord God Almighty. (NIV)

THE FINAL TEST FOR JUDGING REVELATION IS TO examine the fruit. Some fruit is immediate, like the scriptures above—clarity, understanding, joy, or peace. When these things accompany what we hear, there is a higher chance that it did come from God.

But the real test is the long-term fruit.

A number of years ago I was talking with a co-laborer in ministry as we were out sharing the Gospel. I was excited that I had had a dream about current political events and was sharing the dream with him. It was a strange dream with a fairly general, nebulous interpretation.

My friend asked me, "How is that going to change your life?"

I stumbled for an answer. The air went out of my sails. I asked him what he thought.

He answered, "I think you think too highly of yourself."

Faithful are the wounds of a friend. I have thanked him multiple times since then for that rebuke, and apart from the lesson I learned from him and prayer, that dream has never borne fruit.

I've since learned to ask the same question when people tell me they've heard from God. I ask, "How is that going to change your life?" and "What are you going to do about that?" These two questions illuminate whether or not the revelation they received is really going to bear fruit in their lives. Will it really change anything?

God's voice is powerful, and we cannot hear God and stay the same. A true encounter with His voice guarantees transformation. We may not always understand how. There are times when God speaks and the mysteries He reveals don't bear fruit until years later, but most of the time God speaks to us at the right time for us to respond. God's Word does not return void (Isaiah 55:11). It accomplishes its purpose, and it bears fruit in our lives. If the revelation we receive has no impact, it may not be from the Lord at all.

Learning to discern God's voice is a process of trial and error. We think we hear God, we apply the revelation, and we learn—whether or not it bears fruit. Sometimes we miss it and make mistakes—the "word," obviously, does not bear fruit. We don't beat ourselves up, but we do make a correction. "That was not God's voice. I will be careful not to make that mistake again." When we hear God's voice and it does bear fruit, we immediately say, "That was God! I will remember what that was like because that was the voice of the Father." In order to grow and learn in this way we have to be honest about what bore fruit in our lives and what did not. We have to be willing to admit our mistakes.

Many times I've turned down certain streets because I felt that God was directing me to. There have been a number of times when nothing happened. I didn't encounter anyone, there was no testimony from it, and as far as I know there was no purpose to it. It is possible that God told me to do that anyway for some reason I can't see or understand, but I can't confirm that.

There are other times when I turned down a specific street because I felt that God told me to, and I ran into an old friend, met someone who was miraculously healed when I prayed for them, ran into someone who came to Christ when I shared the gospel, or encountered someone who was running from domestic abuse and needed help. These moments are easily confirmed as hearing God accurately because they bore recognizable fruit. I can say, "That *was* God because I see His purpose being fulfilled through my obedience to His voice."

If what we think God said has no application and does not change someone's life, it is suspect.

Often the only way to test God's voice this way is to obey and apply what we think we heard. If you hear God speaking, step out and obey what He says. Apply what He tells you. Then evaluate what fruit comes from your obedience. Correct and adjust when needed, and celebrate when God's word bears fruit.

Prayer Starter:

- ❑ Thank God for the power of His word, which always accomplishes its purpose. Thank God for the power of His voice to produce fruit in your life.
- ❑ Ask God to help you to learn and grow in His voice. Ask God to remind you of areas where following His voice has borne good fruit.
- ❑ Pray that God would bless others and produce fruit and glory for Him and His kingdom as He teaches you to hear His voice.

Journal Experience:

Was there ever a time in your life when God spoke to you or told you to do something and it produced verifiable fruit? Was there ever a time when you made a big mistake when it came to discerning God's voice? What was that like? Write down any lessons you learned (if any) from these experiences. What could you do to avoid making that same mistake in the future?

_____

_____

_____

_____

_____

_____

_____

_____

_____

_____

_____

_____

_____

Action Step:

Ask God to speak to you this week in a testable way. Expect God to answer. When He does, follow through on what God says and test the result. Did it bear good fruit? Even if it doesn't bear fruit, congratulate yourself for your childlike obedience, and take a lesson from the experience. Fruit or no fruit, you have grown in hearing God's voice. Journal every part of the process as soon as possible after it takes place.

Supplemental Reading:
❏   1 Thessalonians 5:21
❏   Isaiah 55

SECTION 5:
How to Respond to Revelation

Day 21
Asking God What to Do

Art Thomas (with James Loruss)

Sometimes God will tell you something about somebody or about a circumstance, but it's not meant to be said. The great question to ask is, "Lord, You showed me this picture of what's going on. Now, what's Your heart about that situation?" That's where you get prophetic words. It always starts with, "God, what's in Your heart?"

~ Kevin Berry

> **Psalm 25:9-10** — He leads the humble in doing right, teaching them His way. The Lord leads with unfailing love and faithfulness all who keep His covenant and obey His demands. (NLT)

THE LORD "LEADS THE HUMBLE IN DOING RIGHT." The Lord leads, and that means we don't. The moment I step ahead of God — putting my desires above His — I'm bound to fail. I need to let God lead.

This doesn't mean we're not allowed to initiate. My wife can always come to me and ask if I want to dance; but as soon as I respond to her initiation, she needs to let me lead or else there will be some sore toes. You can ask God for a word for someone, but then ask Him how to deliver what He showed you. You can ask Him to lead you to someone who needs ministry. But then ask Him when to go and what to say or do when you find the person. You can ask Him to speak to you through the Scriptures, but then ask Him what to do with the revelation you receive. You're allowed to initiate, but God still leads.

It's tempting to hear something from the Lord and immediately assume that we know what we're supposed to do with it. As an evangelist who is often invited to train churches in healing ministry, I've learned that sometimes the most effective training comes from seeing healing in action. Many times the Lord has instructed me to bring one or more people to the front of the room and demonstrate to the church how healing ministry works. Most of the time, if I'm truly following the Holy Spirit, the person is healed in front of everyone. But I've had a number of times when I brought someone up only to have the miracle not happen.

In those moments, I learn that the Lord watches my heart more closely than I do. God "opposes the proud but gives grace to the humble." (See James 4:6.) If I want to remain in His unearned, empowering favor, I need to remain humble. I need to let Him lead.

In some cases, He showed me later that my motives in bringing someone up were to validate myself, not to train the Church. Other times He showed me that I wasn't paying attention to what was happening in the hearts and minds of the congregation—they were starting to put me on a pedestal, and He didn't want them to think they were inferior to me. Still other times, the Lord showed me later that He wanted me to minister in a particular way, and I ran ahead with my "default methods."

After publicly falling on my face several times, I started talking to the Lord about what needs to change in me. Now, if I receive a "word of knowledge" about a condition someone has, my next step is to ask the Lord if He intends for me to call out this condition publicly or quietly approach the person later. After that, I ask if He wants me to demonstrate healing ministry or if He wants someone else to do it. If someone else, I ask *who*. If me, I ask *how*.

I recognize most readers don't find themselves in the same situation, preaching in front of a church. But what about when you're at the grocery store or a restaurant? What about when you're walking down the street or through a parking lot? What do you do if you feel God is giving you a prophetic word or a word of knowledge for somebody out in public? Simple. Ask Him what to do with what He showed you. Talk to Him about it, and He will lead you in doing the right thing at the right moment.

In Acts 9:10-19, Jesus appeared to an ordinary Christian named Ananias and gave him specific instructions about where to find a man named Saul who needed ministry. Ananias recognized the name and realized this "Saul" was the same guy who had been going around killing Christians like him. He questioned the Lord, basically admitting his reluctance. Jesus didn't give up on Ananias. Instead, He gave more detail about Saul's calling and the actions expected of Ananias.

Our dialogue with the Lord leads to greater understanding. Even when the things He has already said are clear, our decision to discuss His words with Him will usually make room for Him to unfold greater detail or further instructions.

Similarly, when it comes to the revelations God gives us as we read His Word, what does He want us to do with what we hear (after we apply it to our own lives, of course)? Should we preach a sermon to a particular group of people? Should we write a song? A blog article? A book? A letter to someone who needs it? Should we journal it and wait until He gives us permission to release it?

Or what if you're in a church meeting and you hear the Lord speak something to you that you feel others would benefit from? Is it actually for everyone else or is it only for you? Ask Him. If it is for everyone else, how and when does He want you to share His words?

Since Paul said in First Corinthians 8:1 that "knowledge puffs up but love builds up," I always ask the Lord, "How can I love with what You've just shown me?" If I can't identify a way to love with it, I scrap it. Any prophetic word that can't be used to love is worthless. Paul calls those who prophesy without love "nothing." (See 1 Corinthians 13:2.)

The very first thing to do when you hear anything from God is to ask Him what He wants you to do with whatever He showed you. Dialogue with Him about it. Ask how, when, where, and other defining questions. You can even ask Him to show you what questions you need to be asking!

As long as your questions are not a veiled attempt at avoiding obedience, they will be beneficial. At some point, though, it's time to act—even if you don't feel ready. The purpose of the questions is not to calm your emotions or make you feel ready. The purpose of the questions is to clarify the mission and define what obedience looks like in this scenario. Rarely will you feel ready to do what God tells you to do. The good news, though, is that Romans 10:17 says "faith comes by hearing." So if you've heard what God is saying, you can trust that you have the faith necessary to follow through. Take a leap, and do what He tells you.

Prayer Starter:

- ☐ Thank Jesus for modeling humility for you and for demonstrating with His earthly life how to depend on the Father and be led by Him.
- ☐ Ask God for a healthy fear of Him and thank Him for confiding in you. Ask Him to uproot any pride or independence in your heart.
- ☐ Ask the Lord to make you more sensitive to His moment-by-moment leading so that you can grow in faith and obedience.

Journal Experience:

Suppose God told you—like Ananias—to go minister healing and share the Gospel with a known terrorist or murderer of Christians. Write a few questions you would ask God before you stepped out in action.

_____

_____

_____

_____

Now, ask the Lord to develop in you the courage and the boldness needed to obey Him no matter the cost. Ask Him what things He wants to teach you (these can be broad topics) that will help you grow in faith and confidence for the future. Write down what comes to mind.

_____

_____

_____

_____

_____

_____

Action Step:

Ask God who He would like you to encourage today. Ask Him what He wants you to say to that person. Dialogue with Him about it until He indicates that you know everything He wants you to know.

Supplemental Reading:
❏   John 15:1-17

DAY 22
ASSESSING RISK LEVELS

Art Thomas

If we want those high-powered, life-changing words from God that will completely right the ship — that will change an entire culture, that will change an entire life, that will change an entire family — then we need to be prepared to receive that kind of word. We need to be prepared to act on that kind of word. We need to have that kind of reverence for the Word of God.

~ *Jonathan Ammon*

1 Kings 22:4-9 — Then [Ahab] turned to Jehoshaphat and asked, "Will you join me in battle to recover Ramoth-gilead?"

Jehoshaphat replied to the king of Israel, "Why, of course! You and I are as one. My troops are your troops, and my horses are your horses." Then Jehoshaphat added, "But first let's find out what the Lord says."

So the king of Israel summoned the

prophets, about 400 of them, and asked them, "Should I go to war against Ramoth-gilead, or should I hold back?"

They all replied, "Yes, go right ahead! The Lord will give the king victory."

But Jehoshaphat asked, "Is there not also a prophet of the Lord here? We should ask him the same question."

The king of Israel replied to Jehoshaphat, "There is one more man who could consult the Lord for us, but I hate him. He never prophesies anything but trouble for me! His name is Micaiah son of Imlah."

Jehoshaphat replied, "That's not the way a king should talk! Let's hear what he has to say."

So the king of Israel called one of his officials and said, "Quick! Bring Micaiah son of Imlah." (NLT)

THIS STORY ABOUT KING AHAB IS A FASCINATING one. Ahab and Jehoshaphat knew that going to war would be a high-risk move, and they didn't want to do it without God's guarantee of victory. That part was good. They consulted people who they trusted to hear from God (today this could be any mature Christian, but back then only some were considered prophetic — unfortunately it appears Ahab and Jehoshaphat were not consulting true, godly prophets). Despite the good report from all those "prophets," Ahab — recognizing the risk — knew there was one other prophet whose voice should be heard. Ahab knowingly brought in someone who frequently spoke against him.

As the rest of the story goes, Micaiah does tell Ahab that all the hundreds of other prophets heard wrong and that the battle was a bad idea. He warns that Ahab will die in battle.

The cautionary tale here, though, is that Ahab was in such rebellion against God that he ignored Micaiah's prophecy and went to battle anyway. The only precaution he took was to dress in a disguise so that the enemy wouldn't target him. But an arrow fired at random hit Ahab between his armor and slowly killed him that same day.

Ahab and Jehoshaphat started out by rightly seeking God for confirmation. They even consulted a prophet who regularly opposed Ahab. Ahab's downfall was primarily caused by his own pride (among other things).

Today, we Christians have the benefit of consulting one another about the things we hear and humbly heeding the caution of even those who frequently contradict us or seem to hold us back. I once wanted to plant a church within the next couple months but chose to first talk to some mature believers who I trust. Everyone seemed to be excited for it and wanting it to happen. Then I thought, *There's one person in my life who might try to stop me, but I trust him to hear God.* Sure enough, this friend pointed out the intensity of my schedule and the grandiosity of my plans and said he was concerned for my well-being and that of my family. He recommended against starting the new church.

I walked away frustrated and thinking he was selfish or had unspoken motives for shutting me down. But then I remembered he cared about me and spoke in love. I decided not to plant the church as planned but to wait—perhaps indefinitely—until the Lord clearly said otherwise.

I'm still waiting, and I don't know when or if

those plans will ever be implemented. But now — in hindsight — I'm so glad I recognized the risk level of what I thought God was speaking and trusted my friend to hear more clearly than me (especially since I was so emotionally engaged in the idea). Far too many situations in my life since then have proven that then was not the time to plant a church.

Not everything you hear needs this level of scrutiny. Some things are low-risk. For example, if you think God is telling you to offer to pray for a stranger at the mall, that's generally a low-risk situation. It may be uncomfortable, but the worst thing that's going to happen is that the person is going to say "no." You're not going to break anything by offering to pray. And even if you didn't hear God, we ought to offer prayer to people anyway! Similarly, God may lead you to encourage another believer. Again, this is safe and doesn't need any confirmation. When the thing you believe God is telling you to do is a low-risk activity like these, just obey immediately and see if it bears fruit.

Some things, however, are what we might consider "moderate risk." Perhaps you feel like God is leading you to do something that could negatively affect your reputation. Or maybe it will cost enough money to put yourself in a difficult or tight financial situation. Perhaps He has given you a corrective word for someone, and that person might reject you or be hurt (especially if you're wrong). In these situations, take a moment to discern. Dialogue with the Lord about it (as we discussed on Day 21), and if helpful, mention it to a Christian friend who will encourage you either to act or reconsider.

Thirdly, we have high-risk situations. Perhaps you feel God is leading you to travel to a foreign country without a church-led team and minister in dangerous places (I do this somewhere in the world about once or twice a year). Or maybe He gave you a prophetic word about who someone will marry, a person having a baby, or some other emotionally-charged topic. If the potential for emotional, relational, physical, or spiritual damage is high (and especially if it could cost you your life), fast and pray until you have clarity. Share with some other seasoned Christians, and ask them to help you discern. Perhaps even run the idea by some believers who you suspect will tell you not to do it. If they're behind you, the odds are greater that you're doing the right thing. And finally, proceed with caution. Don't be afraid to tell people, "I'm not sure whether or not I'm hearing this from God..."

As you walk with the Lord and learn His voice over time, your "risk tolerance" will change. Things that used to seem like high-risk matters may become moderate risks or even low risks if history has proven that God often speaks to you accurately in these ways. Romans 12:6 tells us to prophesy "in proportion" to our faith. As your faith grows, so will your threshold for risk.

Prayer Starter:

- ❑ Thank God for His faithfulness and trustworthiness.
- ❑ Ask the Lord to increase your measure of faith and to expand your capacity for greater prophetic words.

❏ Ask the Holy Spirit to help you manage the tension between humility and boldness. Ask Him to challenge you to reach out to others in ways that are new or uncomfortable to you.

Journal Experience:

Ask God to grow your faith for high-risk obedience. Ask Him to encourage you and help you to see Him the way He sees you. Ask, "God, what do you want me to remember about myself or learn about myself that I'm not seeing clearly right now?" Write down what comes to mind.

_____

_____

_____

_____

_____

_____

_____

_____

Action Step:

Ask the Holy Spirit to raise your risk tolerance and to tell you something to do today that you can handle but that perhaps pushes you beyond what is normally comfortable for you. Then follow through.

Day 23
Humbling Yourself with a Personal Response

Art Thomas (with James Loruss)

When you feel God tells you something – out of scripture, or an encounter, or a life situation – sometimes there is a temptation to immediately think that He gave us a message for someone else. But I would encourage you that if you just sit with it for a while, it may actually be something that He wants to speak to you… And later on it can become a message that you release.

~ Philip Schmerold

> **Romans 2:21-24** — Well then, if you teach others, why don't you teach yourself? You tell others not to steal, but do you steal? You say it is wrong to commit adultery, but do you commit adultery? You condemn idolatry, but do you use items stolen from pagan temples? You are so proud of knowing the

law, but you dishonor God by breaking it.
No wonder the Scriptures say, "The
Gentiles blaspheme the name of God
because of you." (NLT)

BEFORE DELIVERING A PROPHETIC WORD TO
someone else, first consider that message for
yourself. Some people have such a low view of
themselves that the encouragement God pours into
them is ejected before it can be absorbed. I can think
of times when I heard someone share a prophetic
word in a church meeting and thought to myself,
"The person in this room who needs to hear that
most is the one who said it!"

The same applies for words of instruction or
correction. As the old saying goes, "practice what
you preach." If you're ever excited to bring a
corrective word to someone, chances are you may be
in pride yourself. In Romans 2:1, we read, "You,
therefore, have no excuse, you who pass judgment
on someone else, for at whatever point you judge
another, you are condemning yourself, because you
who pass judgment do the same things."

Jesus spoke to this issue as well. "Why do you
look at the speck of sawdust in your brother's eye
and pay no attention to the plank in your own eye?
How can you say to your brother, 'Let me take the
speck out of your eye,' when all the time there is a
plank in your own eye? You hypocrite, first take the
plank out of your own eye, and then you will see
clearly to remove the speck from your brother's eye"
(Matthew 7:3-5).

Jesus gives us license to correct, but only with
plank-free eyes. Our goal should be freedom—not
only for them but for us as well. The whole point of

bringing a word of correction is to bring wholeness and freedom, not condemnation and guilt. If we truly love someone, bringing a correction—although healthy—should not be a pleasant experience for us.

Philippians 2:4 (AMP) says, "Do not merely look out for your own personal interests, but also for the interests of others." Jesus was (and is) the Master of the balance between truth and love. He never compromises either one because (1) He is The Truth, and (2) He embodies love. (See John 14:6 and 1 John 4:16.) In the same way, everything we do should be with the posture of love and humility.

Sometimes we look at the sin in our nation, or city, or even our church or family, and we begin to feel a measure of what God feels regarding that issue. A mix of love-sick, righteous anger and heartbrokenness well up in our hearts, and we become aware that the Holy Spirit is grieved over that matter. From that place, we become aware that God has things to say about the problem, and we start to consider what our roles might be in warning others.

A great example in my own home country of America is the topic of abortion. Hundreds of thousands of infant lives are needlessly ended in the name of convenience every year, and the Church at large has rightly taken up their cause (though there may be disagreements about the best ways to address it).

But how many of us are vocal about ending abortion while personally bowing to a "spirit of abortion" in our own lives? We may not be guilty of aborting pregnancies, but we are guilty of aborting our marriages, our families, our churches, our jobs, our friendships, and more—all in the name of convenience. We abort our God-given dreams, callings, and ministries because of fear for the future. We abort family time to watch television or engage in our hobbies. We abort relationships with emotionally struggling people because we don't want them to bring us down. We do essentially the same thing as the abortion clinics, just in a different way.

When the somber weightiness of God's grief for the unborn begins to stir in your heart, ask the Holy Spirit if there are any God-given things in your life that you have needlessly aborted.

Let the Lord expose and uproot any issues in your own life that mirror the thing you want to address. As the victory of Jesus is applied to our lives in an area, our prophetic voice for that thing begins to carry more weight. People seem to somehow recognize that we have authority to speak to these issues because we are not bowing to those same issues in other ways.

When God speaks encouragement to you, let it sink into your own heart first. Then prophesy out of the overflow. When God gives you a word of correction for someone, first see if it applies to your own life. Address it in your own heart first and then humbly prophesy out of the overflow. When God gives you a revelation or a word of instruction from which you think others would benefit, put it into action in your own life first and then share it out of the overflow. Our mouths naturally speak what overflows from our hearts. (See Luke 6:45.)

It is important to note that I'm not saying we need to be worthy to deliver a prophetic word. No one is technically qualified. We speak because God entrusted the message to us, regardless of whether or not we feel like we measure up. He gave us the message because He loves and trusts us, not because He considered us "good enough." All I am saying is that we don't want to share what God has to say for others and miss out on a personal application. It would be sad to prophetically minister freedom to a group of people and be the only one in the room still trapped.

Nevertheless, purity of heart does still add weight to our words—even if only in the minds of others. Often the most impactful prophetic words come from people whose lifestyles already proclaim the message before they open their mouths.

Prayer Starter:

- ❏ Thank God for His mercy and His patience with you when you were still a sinner.
- ❏ Ask the Lord to remove any planks from your eyes—to expose and uproot anything in your life that is hindering you from seeing clearly.
- ❏ Ask God to help you minister to others with humility, reverence, and a pure heart.

Journal Experience:

Ask Father God if there is anything He wants to correct in your heart right now. Write down any problem areas He shows you. Ask Him what He wants to say about those issues, and journal what you sense Him saying.

_____

_____

_____

_____

_____

_____

_____

_____

_____

_____

_____

_____

_____

_____

_____

_____

Action Step:

Ask another Christian who you trust to identify one thing they see in your life that is not like Jesus and could be changed. Ask them to pray for you right away regarding that issue.

Supplemental Reading:
❑   Romans 5:8
❑   John 8:1-11

DAY 24
HOW TO SHARE REVELATION WITH OTHERS

Art Thomas (with James Loruss)

It needs to be done in humility. I prefer that we don't have to use King James English – I actually discourage people from doing that. We don't have to change our voice or do a certain position or stance.

~ Randy Clark

> 1 Corinthians 14:31-33 — For you can all prophesy in turn so that everyone may be instructed and encouraged. The spirits of prophets are subject to the control of prophets. For God is not a God of disorder but of peace—as in all the congregations of the Lord's people. (NIV)

CERTAIN PRINCIPLES GUIDE MY LIFE AND MINISTRY. They all boil down to attempting to be like Jesus, and that can only happen through obedience and love. Whatever I do—whether I prophesy, teach, heal, etc — it has to been done out of love.

But love doesn't always rule the day in our churches. Sometimes we bypass love for the sake of fitting in with the Pentecostal or Charismatic culture around us. The result is usually that those already within our culture are unfazed while any newcomers or unbelievers think we're out of our minds.

Some people add certain theatrics to their prophecies like Shakespearean English (thee, thy, thou…), extra syllables ("Open-*uh* your eyes-*uh*…"), abnormal physical behavior (shaking, wobbling, rocking, shouting, screaming, etc.), or divine signatures ("Thus saith the Lord God"). These things can happen for one of a few reasons. In the most innocent of cases (which may even be most cases), this is how prophetic ministry was modeled to that person, and they simply don't know any better. Another possibility is insecurity. Some people are so insecure that they don't believe people will take their words seriously unless they're super theatrical or have a vividly described vision or dream to accompany it. There are also, unfortunately, some people out there who are straight-up false prophets dealing in deception, and the theatrics are their way of psychologically manipulating their audiences into believing their act.

That said, it is also worth noting that God can indeed work in these ways, and perhaps that's how all these behaviors started. The Old and New Testaments of the Bible both contain examples of what I have called "divine signatures" where the prophet emphatically declares that God is speaking. It's not uncommon to see biblical examples of people prophesying "in a loud voice" (though this probably has more to do with the need to reach the ears of a large audience without an electronic sound system than it has to do with being a necessary component of prophecy). And occasionally strange behaviors or theatrics did accompany a word from the Lord. But all of these things in the Bible seem to be appropriate for the moment and right for their audience. There are also examples of calm, relational, and down-to-earth prophecies (like the prophet Nathan in Second Samuel 12:1-14).

First Corinthians 14:32 says, "The spirits of prophets are subject to the control of the prophets." Having a word from God—while it may make you excited—should not make you out of control. The "fruit of the Spirit" includes self-control. (See Galatians 5:22-23.) No matter how good your word from God is, if it's not delivered with self-control, then it's not being done in union with His Spirit. I find it hard to believe that God will give you something to say that is so profound that He breaks His character. Don't disregard His nature in the name of prophecy. That doesn't make any sense.

When God gives you a prophetic word, take a moment to assess risk levels, humble yourself with a personal response, and ask God what to do with it. Take whatever precautions are reasonable, and when you feel confident that you're supposed to step out (even if you don't feel confident to actually do it), ask the Lord how He wants you to deliver the word.

God's delivery method will be appropriate for the audience—even if it seems strange to you. All that matters is that we are walking in union with the Lord, delivering His words with His nature, His heart, and His methods. What we're avoiding is any sort of delivery method that might be based on our own personal insecurities or a desire to be praised or known. Keep your eyes on Jesus and deliver the word with humility.

Methods of delivery are not limited to speech. The prophetic words of Scripture were largely written (though some are written records of spoken words), so you may feel led to write your prophetic word. Ezekiel made a physical model of his prophetic word. (See Ezekiel 4.) Hosea married a promiscuous woman as part of delivering a prophetic word. I don't recommend this in today's culture, but Isaiah actually walked around naked as a sort of object lesson connected to his prophetic word. (See Isaiah 20.) The common element among all of these deliveries—especially the really strange ones—is that all of them were done under the direction of the Lord. It's not like God gave a word and the prophet tried to figure out the most provocative way to deliver it. Like the words themselves, the prophets' delivery methods also came from dialogue with the Lord.

Under God's direction, you could draw or paint a prophetic word. You might deliver it in song—either rehearsed or spontaneously. You could act it out with a prop like the prophet Agabus. (See Acts 21:10-11.) You might make a model or build a structure. What matters is obedience.

It's just as important to evaluate, "What is God saying?" as it is, "How would God say this?" Our God is a God of adventure and fun. He's wild and unpredictable at times, but He is not disorderly. He is intentional. We—the body of Christ—should strive to be the same as we obediently represent Him in love.

Prayer Starter:

- ❏ Thank God for being the author of love. Take a moment to worship Him for His loving wisdom and orderliness.
- ❏ Ask God if there's any area where you've been misrepresenting Him. Take time to receive His correction, repent, and receive His quick forgiveness.
- ❏ Ask God to help you love like He does. Ask Him to make clear to you the right ways to deliver what He is saying when He speaks.

Journal Experience:

Ask the Lord to bring to your mind one person in your life who He wants to speak to. Write down their name below, and then begin to write down whatever you sense Him saying about them.

_____

_____

_____

_____

_____

_____

_____

_____

_____

_____

_____

_____

_____

_____

_____

_____

_____

_____

_____

_____

_____

_____

_____

_____

_____

Action Step:

Ask God what He wants you to do with what you wrote in today's Journal Experience. Does He want you to share it? If so, how and when? Once you know, follow through.

Supplemental Reading:
❑   2 Samuel 12:1-14
❑   1 Corinthians 2

DAY 25
WHEN NOT TO SHARE REVELATION

Art Thomas

Out of that place, you learn the most important thing a prophetic person or a prophet can know: When to be quiet. So there's time to speak, there's time to minister, but there's time to be quiet.

~ *Justin Allen*

> **Daniel 8:26** — "This vision about the 2,300 evenings and mornings is true. But none of these things will happen for a long time, so keep this vision a secret." (NLT)
>
> **2 Corinthians 12:2,4** — I know a man in Christ who fourteen years ago was caught up to the third heaven....and heard inexpressible things, things that no one is permitted to tell. (NIV)
>
> **Revelation 10:4** — And when the seven thunders spoke, I was about to

write; but I heard a voice from heaven
say, "Seal up what the seven thunders
have said and do not write it down." (NIV)

KNOWING GOD IS SOMETIMES LIKE BEING MARRIED.
There are a lot of conversations and shared
experiences I have had with my wife that we can
both share freely and openly. But there are also
conversations and shared experiences that are for us
alone. That's the definition of "intimacy."

Sometimes God reveals secret things to us
simply because He loves us and not because He
wants us to say them or do anything about it. I
remember the very first heavenly encounter I ever
had and the Lord telling me three people I was
allowed to tell about it (and no one else). I remember
two election years when God told me who would be
elected president in the United States—not so that I
could proclaim it but simply because I asked Him.

Similarly, I've had multiple heavenly
encounters, but I've only felt a release from the Lord
to talk about a few of them (and even those with
limited detail).

In general, there are three reasons not to share
something the Lord reveals to you: (1) Obedience,
(2) Intimacy, and (3) Love.

First, *obedience.* If God tells you not to say
anything about what He showed you, then don't say
anything. That one's simple.

Second, *intimacy.* If God hasn't told you
whether or not to share what He has shown you,
then He is likely giving you the option to either share
it or keep it as a matter of intimacy. There's nothing
wrong with sharing when God hasn't told you not to.
But there is value in holding things near to your

heart either indefinitely or until a time that seems appropriate. In Luke 2:19, after the shepherds described the host of angels proclaiming her son's birth, we learn that "Mary treasured up all these things and pondered them in her heart." It may not have been until Luke came along, trying to write his "orderly account" of Jesus' life (Luke 1:1-4), that Mary finally opened up that treasure chest of experiences from Jesus' birth. Not everything we know needs to be shared.

Finally, *love*. What is your reason for sharing? Is it that you want attention? Do you want to impress people with your Bible knowledge or insight? Do you want people to celebrate you for your prophetic experiences? Or are you truly wanting to help people in ways that will actually be beneficial to them? In John 16:12, Jesus said, "I have much more to say to you, more than you can now bear." The things Jesus wanted to say were good and beneficial things, but He knew the disciples would be overwhelmed if He shared all of it. Love for His friends constrained Him from sharing.

As mentioned in a previous lesson, I have spent years trying to fully conquer a bad habit. Whenever someone tells me about a revelation they've had out of Scripture, I often want to engage in conversation by sharing what I've learned about that topic as well. Years ago, though, my pastor pointed out to me that while my intentions are good, people often walk away thinking I was trying to one-up their revelation—as though I was either telling them that their revelation was inferior or even outright wrong.

While I occasionally still slip up in that area, I have tried intently to "rejoice with those who rejoice" and not try to add anything to what the person is saying (unless they actually ask for my thoughts). The reason is simple: love. I want the people around me to feel valued, not inferior.

When I lead small group meetings, I encourage everyone to join the conversation. And I also encourage everyone not to dominate the conversation. I say, "Each one of us—myself included—ought to value the revelations Jesus has given others more than we value our own. Why? Because we already know what He has revealed to us, but we don't know what He has revealed to others. So share what you have (because we all value that), but try to keep it concise so that you have time to hear from everyone else too." As Romans 12:10 says, "Honor one another above yourselves."

If God tells you not to share something, it's either because He is purposefully engaging in intimacy with you or because He knows that the time isn't right, that others can't handle it, or that sharing it would trap you in pride.

But when God doesn't tell you whether or not to share something, then He likely wants to see how you will steward what He has given you. Will you "treasure it in your heart" or "cast your pearls before swine?" (See Luke 2:19 and Matthew 7:6.) Will you keep it secret as a matter of intimacy or will you make a show of it, hoping to boost your image or how others think of you? On the other side of the coin, will you bury your talent or will you faithfully share a word in season? (See Matthew 25:14-30 and Proverbs 25:11.) There's no wrong way to do it or not do it, as long as your motivation is love.

Proverbs 25:11 (CEV) says, "The right word at the right time is like precious gold set in silver."

Prayer Starter:

- ❑ Thank God for His desire to be intimate with you.
- ❑ Ask the Holy Spirit to shape you more and more into someone who can be fully trusted with the secrets of His heart.
- ❑ Ask the Lord to make you more aware of what will be most beneficial to the people around you. Ask Him to help you love like He does.

Journal Experience:

Take a moment to engage in intimacy with the Lord. Write Him a short, worshipful "love note." Briefly tell Him what He means to you. And when you're done, ask Him if there's anything He wants you to know about how He sees you. Write that too.

_____

_____

_____

_____

_____

_____

_____

_____

_____

_____

_____

_____

_____

_____

_____

_____

_____

_____

_____

Action Step:

Go to a fellow believer (perhaps a friend or pastor) who you consider to be successful in sharing revelation with others — someone who bears lasting fruit in the Kingdom. Ask them for their top three tips about knowing what to say, when to say it, and how to deliver it. If they know you well enough to offer constructive feedback, also ask them if there are any specific ways you can improve in your own delivery of the things God has revealed to you. Ask them to pray for you to effectively share revelation with others.

Supplemental Reading:
❑   Matthew 6:1-18

SECTION 6:
Knowing God through His Voice

DAY 26
GOD REVEALS HIS NATURE THROUGH HIS VOICE

Jonathan Ammon

God says He's compassionate, He's merciful, He's slow to anger, He's abounding in love, He's full of truth and trustworthiness, and lastly He's a just God.

~ *Jeremiah Johnson*

> **Exodus 34:5-7a** — Then the Lord came down in the cloud and stood there with him and proclaimed His name, the Lord. And He passed in front of Moses, proclaiming, "The Lord, the Lord, the compassionate and gracious God, slow to anger, abounding in love and faithfulness, maintaining love to thousands, and forgiving wickedness, rebellion and sin. Yet He does not leave the guilty unpunished... (NIV)

COMMUNICATION IS HOW WE LEARN WHO SOMEONE is, what they think, and what they feel. Communication is the primary way we experience another person. God's communication with us is the primary way we experience Him. This includes reading His word to us in Scripture, experiencing His presence in worship, or hearing His voice in other ways. Every time we hear God's voice we gain a better understanding of who He is.

"[T]he things that come out of a person's mouth come from the heart..." (Matthew 15:18). What God speaks comes from God's heart. His voice is the voice of love and grace and reveals His love and grace to us. His voice is loving, joyful, and peaceful. It is the voice of longsuffering and patience. His voice is full of goodness and faithfulness. His voice is gentle and controlled. (See Galatians 5:22-23.) We can recognize God's voice because it sounds like His nature. It sounds like the fruit of the Spirit and love.

Every encounter we have with God's voice increases our knowledge of Him. And it is a personal knowledge. We aren't learning about God; we are experiencing Him as He is. Our experiences are not always perfect — we still see through a glass darkly (1 Corinthians 13:12), but God reveals Himself to us in intimate ways revealing the reality of His nature in a language that is perfect for us.

Every word from God is a revelation of God. We see His character, His nature, and His glory. As we gaze into it, we are transformed. "And we all, who with unveiled faces contemplate the Lord's glory, are being transformed into His image with ever-increasing glory, which comes from the Lord, who is the Spirit" (2 Corinthians 3:18). God meets us to reveal Himself. He wants us to know Him on an intimate level, and He desires to reveal His nature to us. As we experience Him, we conform to His beauty and His love. We are His children. We have received His nature. And when we hear His voice, we know that nature in action. We imitate our Father as the knowledge of Him reveals who we are meant to be.

You cannot know God without hearing His voice. The more we hear, the more we are transformed. God desires us to know Him, and knowing Him — glorifying Him through a love relationship — should be the goal of our lives.

Prayer Starter:

❑ Thank God for revealing Himself to us through Jesus. Thank God for His character.
❑ Ask God to give you a greater desire to know Him and interact with Him for fellowship.
❑ Ask God to reveal Himself and His character to others through you.

Journal Experience:

Has God ever spoken to you in a way that changed the way you knew and understood Him? What was that like? What did you learn?

_____

_____

_____

_____

_____

_____

_____

_____

_____

What does God's voice feel like when you hear it? What have you learned about God from hearing His voice?

_____

_____

_____

_____

_____

_____

Action Step:

Ask God to speak to you right now about who He is. Ask Him to reveal something about Himself and to teach you something about Himself in a new way. Listen carefully and record what He says and how He says it. What is God's communication like? Bold? Patient? What can you learn from that?

Supplemental Reading:
- ❏ 1 Corinthians 13
- ❏ Galatians 5:22-26

DAY 27
JESUS IS THE WORD OF GOD

James Loruss (with Art Thomas)

If you can't imagine Jesus saying what you're saying, you're not saying the right thing.

~ *JonMark Baker*

John 1:1-5,14 — In the beginning was the Word, and the Word was with God, and the Word was God. He was with God in the beginning. Through Him all things were made; without Him nothing was made that has been made. In Him was life, and that life was the light of all mankind. The light shines in the darkness, and the darkness has not overcome it.... The Word became flesh and made His dwelling among us. We have seen His glory, the glory of the one and only Son, who came from the Father, full of grace and truth. (NIV)

> **Hebrews 1:1-3a** — In the past God spoke to our ancestors through the prophets at many times and in various ways, but in these last days He has spoken to us by His Son, whom He appointed heir of all things, and through whom also He made the universe. The Son is the radiance of God's glory and the exact representation of His being, sustaining all things by His powerful word… (NIV)

IF YOU WANT TO KNOW GOD'S HEART, LOOK AT Jesus. If you want to know truth, look at Jesus. If you want to see God's glory, look at Jesus.

John 1 is a profound scripture. In a culture seeking knowledge and truth, John comes along and personifies truth in a Man. Jesus is the embodiment of truth. Not only does Jesus speak the words of God, but He actually *IS* the Word of God.

All through Scripture we see God's voice carrying His will and His presence. Psalm 33:4-6 says, "For the word of the Lord is right and true; He is faithful in all He does. The Lord loves righteousness and justice; the earth is full of His unfailing love. By the word of the Lord the heavens were made, their starry host by the breath of His mouth." God's voice is inseparable from who He is.

Many have been confused by the idea of the Trinity—Father, Son, and Holy Spirit—being three distinct persons and yet perfectly "one." I won't pretend to solve everything for you in a couple paragraphs, but the following analogy might help you think about things better:

Jesus—even before being conceived in Mary—has always (for eternity) proceeded from the Father. He has always been the Word of God. When I hear someone's voice—perhaps on a telephone or in another room—I can identify who it is. And yet, what I am experiencing is the person's voice and not the physical person themself. It *is* them, but it is also, in a sense, *not* technically them. It is their voice. Their voice is completely inseparable from who they are. My voice is completely me even though it is only an expression of me.

In the same way, Jesus is completely God—the perfect expression of the Father, proceeding from His heart and accomplishing His will. God's voice is inseparable from who He is. Yes, there is technically a distinction between the Speaker and His Voice, but they are still perfectly One—the Voice revealing the heart of the Speaker.

Luke 6:45 says that "the mouth speaks what the heart is full of." Just as our mouths will spill out whatever is in our hearts, Jesus—the Word of God—is the overflow of the Father's heart. Whenever God speaks, Jesus is revealed. And whenever Jesus is revealed, we gain a clearer understanding of the Father—the One who spoke. Jesus said, "Anyone who has seen Me has seen the Father" (John 14:9).

When you spend time being aware of God's presence and draw near to Him, He will speak to you. What He speaks is inseparable from who He is. What He speaks is a revelation of Jesus, made known to us by the Holy Spirit. Jesus said, "But when He, the Spirit of truth, comes, He will guide you into all the truth. He will not speak on His own; He will speak only what He hears...He will glorify Me because it is from Me that He will receive what He will make known to you. All that belongs to the Father is Mine. That is why I said the Spirit will receive from Me what He will make known to you"

(John 16:13-15). In other words, The Holy Spirit makes Jesus known to us—little by little—and all of it is technically also a revelation of the Father.

When it comes to prophetic ministry, what we speak is a revelation of Jesus. Revelation 19:10 says that "it is the Spirit of prophecy who bears testimony to Jesus." When the Holy Spirit empowers us to speak prophetically, we speak as part of Jesus' body in the earth, revealing Him to those around us. (See 1 Corinthians 12.) There is no such thing as a true prophetic word that does not somehow make Jesus known.

Finally, remember we have been crucified with Christ, and we no longer live, but Christ lives in us (Galatians 2:20). If true, then we too are designed to be expressions of God to the world—only through the life-giving work of the Holy Spirit, of course. Jesus is the perfect expression of the Father, and we are being conformed into His image from one degree of glory to the next (2 Corinthians 3:18). As the Holy Spirit transforms our lives to look more and more like Jesus, we actually become living, breathing prophetic words to the world. In 2 Corinthians 3:3, Paul writes, "You show that you are a letter from Christ...written not with ink but with the Spirit of the living God..."

You are a prophecy—a letter from Christ—a work of the Spirit who reveals Jesus and expresses the Father's heart. And if that is true, what ought we expect to be the overflow of your heart? Jesus. That means even your everyday, ordinary speech ought to have a prophetic weightiness to it as the nature of God is revealed through what you say and how you say it.

Prayer Starter:

- ❑ Thank God for revealing Himself through Jesus. Praise Him for inviting you into fellowship with Him and making you an expression of His heart.
- ❑ Ask God if you've been misrepresenting Jesus with your words, actions, or attitudes. If He shows you anything that needs to change, surrender it to Him. Ask the Holy Spirit to help you think and live differently.
- ❑ Make a fresh expression of surrender to the Holy Spirit, asking Him to continue to produce Christ's life in you so that others around you can experience God.

Journal Experience:

In Episode 1 of our two-part film series, *Voice of God*, we asked many of our interview subjects to describe Jesus to us. If you've seen it, you will remember the lengthy and worshipful segment as one person after the next lovingly exalted Jesus. Now it's your turn. Describe Jesus. Let your heart be drawn into worship as you write His attributes.

_____

_____

_____

_____

_____

_____

_____

_____

_____

_____

_____

_____

_____

_____

_____

_____

_____

Action Step:

Meditate on the truth that Jesus' physical body was God's presence on the earth, and now, according to First Corinthians 12:27, you are a part of the body of Christ. And it's not just a metaphor. First Corinthians 6:15 asks, "Do you not know that your bodies are members of Christ Himself?" We were actually designed to be physical expressions of Jesus.

As you contemplate these truths, ask Jesus how He wants to move in your sphere of influence today. Ask Him what plans are in His heart that include you.

Supplemental Reading:
❑ John 14:5-14
❑ 1 Corinthians 12

DAY 28
ENCOUNTERING GOD THROUGH THE REVELATIONS HE HAS GIVEN TO OTHERS

Art Thomas

And sometimes we need someone from the outside to come in with that clear, prophetic voice.

~ *Jennifer LeClaire*

> **1 Corinthians 14:29** — Two or three prophets should speak, and the others should weigh carefully what is said. (NIV)

JESUS WANTS YOU TO ENCOUNTER HIM BECAUSE THE more we encounter Him, the more we become like Him. And the more we become like Him, the more we reveal Him. And the more we reveal Him, the more others can encounter Him. This is how the Kingdom of God multiplies.

Now, if it is true that others can encounter God through us, then it also stands to reason that we can encounter God through others.

On Day 14 we talked about "Listening to Others" as a way of positioning ourselves to receive revelation from God. We learned that the Church is a prophetic people and that we all can speak on His behalf. And we learned that by being open to what others have to say, we can hear from God through them.

But today I want to take things further — not only learning from others or listening to what they say but actually encountering God in the midst of it.

In speaking of Jesus' return, John writes, "But we know that when Christ appears, we shall be like Him, for we shall see Him as He is." Of course this refers to a future event, but the principle is relevant today: The more clearly I can see Him, the more like Him I become. Similarly Second Corinthians 3:18 says, "And we all, who with unveiled faces contemplate the Lord's glory, are being transformed into His image with ever-increasing glory, which comes from the Lord, who is the Spirit."

As we behold Him, we become like Him. As we take the time to contemplate His glory, we are transformed to look more like Him. So it is one thing to hear another believer say something and think, *Ooh. That's good;* but it's another thing to (1) realize that whatever good came from them is an expression of Jesus, (2) take time to behold His wisdom, and (3) allow that truth to sink deeply into your own heart and transform you.

God doesn't give revelation to His children to merely affect our minds. He gives it to transform us. Romans 12:2 commands us to "be transformed by the renewing of your mind." Here Paul indicates that "new thinking" is only half of the equation. The second half is surrendering to the transformation process that this new thinking is able to produce.

As people share what God is speaking to them, it does in fact influence the way we think. Paul told the Corinthians church that he was ready to preach to them in such a way that their wrong thoughts would be taken captive and corrected (2 Corinthians 10:1-6). The revelations of God spoken through others have the capacity to "demolish arguments" in our minds and shatter "every pretension that sets itself up against the knowledge of God" (2 Corinthians 10:5). We *need* to hear what God is speaking through others.

When someone shares with you something that they believe God showed them, you have a biblical responsibility to "weigh carefully what is said" (1 Corinthians 14:29). That doesn't simply mean that your job is to give a thumbs-up or a thumbs-down—a "pass" or "fail"—based on how you feel. The Greek word used here invites us to wrestle with the word and even oppose it in our minds until we determine whether or not it is valid. This is where we apply the methods of judging revelation that we studied in Section 4 of this book (Days 16-20).

If we fail to subject everything people share to this level of scrutiny, we leave ourselves vulnerable to believing absolutely everything. We soon start to behold fraudulent ministers and lying spirits rather than beholding Jesus. And if we become what we behold, what do you suppose will be reproduced?

On the other hand, Paul warns us, "Do not quench the Spirit. Do not treat prophecies with contempt but test them all; hold on to what is good, reject every kind of evil" (1 Thessalonians 5:19-22). It does us no good to put our walls so high up that we won't even consider a prophetic word from someone else. Far too many in the Body of Christ treat prophecies with contempt and refuse to even consider that God might truly speak through His people today. Similar to what Bill Johnson said in Episode 2 of *Voice of God*, if there were no such thing as true prophecies, then God wouldn't have had to warn us of the false. If none were true, then we wouldn't be instructed to scrutinize them.

We have to actually test them all—even the ones that anger us, frustrate us, or make us feel uncomfortable. Many times I have tested what I thought was a bogus word and then stood amazed to see that God had indeed spoken. Yes, we are to reject everything that doesn't stand up to scrutiny, but we are to "hold fast" to everything that passes the test.

Many times I have heard revelations from others that were a mixed bag. Perhaps 90% of what they said passed the tests. As the old saying goes, "Chew the meat and spit out the bones." Take what is good and reject the rest. This is common with books, sermons, and other lengthy teachings. We all "know in part and prophesy in part." Try not to hold such impossible standards for your fellow believers that you can never receive anything from God through them. Instead, do as Paul commanded and, "in humility value others above yourselves" (Philippians 2:3). Respond to the revelations of others the way you want people to respond to the revelations God gives you (Matthew 7:12). Allow room for growth, and cherish everything that passes Biblical scrutiny.

Finally, Paul warned Timothy that "the time will come when people will not put up with sound doctrine. Instead, to suit their own desires, they will gather around them a great number of teachers to say what their itching ears want to hear." Be careful to listen to a wide range of Christians from various backgrounds. If what they say doesn't pass the tests, then reject it. But don't reject the people. Be careful that you don't favor division in the Body of Christ by only listening to Christians who already agree with you. Some Christian denominations carry certain revelations of Jesus better than others. We all need to experience and learn from those things.

The more clearly you can see Him, the more fully you will be like Him. Test it all, but take the time to encounter God in the things that pass the test. He will transform you.

Prayer Starter:

- ❑ Take a moment to "behold" Jesus in your heart. Contemplate Him and express your love to Him.
- ❑ Ask God if you have any walls up in your heart that would prevent you from receiving what He speaks through others.
- ❑ Thank God for specific Christians you know (considering several by name) who have revealed His heart to you through their words and actions.

Journal Experience:

Think of someone you know who you feel represents Jesus well. Write down some of the character traits and activities that led you to choose this person.

_____

_____

_____

_____

_____

_____

_____

_____

_____

_____

_____

_____

_____

_____

_____

_____

_____

_____

_____

_____

_____

_____

_____

_____

_____

_____

_____

_____

_____

_____

_____

_____

_____

_____

_____

_____

_____

Now take time to worship Jesus for being the perfect example of those things. Take time to "behold Him" as you contemplate these descriptions of who He is. Ask God to reveal those attributes through you.

Action Step:

Find a Christian who belongs to a different "stream" of Christianity than you do. This could mean they attend a church of a different denomination or perhaps they don't hold the same views about the power of the Holy Spirit as you. As long as they agree that Jesus is Lord, they qualify (even better if they happen to be a pastor or priest who truly represents that other group well).

Next, ask them what is the latest thing God has taught them (whether through the Scriptures, a sermon, or a life experience). Thank them, encourage them, and take time to "weigh carefully" what they said. Take whatever you see of Jesus there, and ask God to apply it to your life.

Supplemental Reading:
❑   1 Corinthians 14:23-33
❑   2 Corinthians 10:1-6

DAY 29
CORRECTION AND DISCIPLINE ARE A FORM OF EMBRACE

Jonathan Ammon (with Art Thomas)

Even when I mess up, God says, "Come on, you know better than this. You can do better than this. You're My son." He doesn't point a finger and say, "Well, what's wrong with you?" He doesn't turn His back on you and say, "That's it! I'm cutting you off!" No. God says, "Listen. You're My son. You know you did wrong. I've already forgiven you. Come on. Let Me work in your life. Come to Me. I'm your Father. It's okay. Let's get back going."

~ *Joe Funaro*

> **Hebrews 12:5-11** — And have you completely forgotten this word of encouragement that addresses you as a father addresses his son? It says,
>
> "My son, do not make light of the

> Lord's discipline,
>   and do not lose heart when He
> rebukes you,
>   because the Lord disciplines
> the one He loves,
>   and He chastens everyone He
> accepts as His son."

Endure hardship as discipline; God is treating you as His children. For what children are not disciplined by their father? If you are not disciplined—and everyone undergoes discipline—then you are not legitimate, not true sons and daughters at all. Moreover, we have all had human fathers who disciplined us and we respected them for it. How much more should we submit to the Father of spirits and live! They disciplined us for a little while as they thought best; but God disciplines us for our good, in order that we may share in His holiness. No discipline seems pleasant at the time, but painful. Later on, however, it produces a harvest of righteousness and peace for those who have been trained by it. (NIV)

WHEN I WAS IN COLLEGE I USED TO PRAY FOR THE campus ministry every morning. I began to pray for my campus pastor. I was unhappy about several of the decisions he had made and several of the things that were going on. I was certain that if different decisions were made, "revival" would break out. But my campus pastor and his decisions stood in the way. In truth, pride had clouded my thinking.

As I sat praying about this, the Lord interrupted my prayers and said very clearly, "I will tell Pastor Jim what to do in his ministry long before I tell you." It was a profound rebuke that has stayed with me for the rest of my life. Judging and critiquing ministries is a common past-time in the church, but God's words to me have echoed in my head since. God speaks to those in leadership about guiding their ministries in a way that He will rarely speak to those outside of leadership. God most often speaks to us about our responsibilities rather than the responsibilities of others.

This rebuke humbled me, but I found an immediate joy in it. I was young in the Lord and so excited to hear God's voice that it almost didn't bother me that I had been wrong. I received the rebuke hungrily and confessed to Pastor Jim what had happened, telling him that I trusted him.

Rebuke, discipline, and correction are signs that we are in God's family. They are evidence that God is taking responsibility for us and our lives—that God is interacting with us. The conviction of the Holy Spirit and the pain of our conscience when we stray are evidences of our new nature and that we belong somewhere else. We belong in righteousness and holiness.

It is often easier to discern God's voice when He corrects us. Most of us do not go out of our way to chasten ourselves. We tend to have confidence in our own opinions and actions. When God speaks to those attitudes and actions to correct them, we know we are hearing something that we would not usually think or acknowledge. It takes humility to receive rebuke, and it also takes security in the love of God.

After God's rebuke I could have responded the way many children respond when they misbehave. I could have denied it, "I didn't do that,

God." Or I could have sunk into despair and hid from God, afraid of His displeasure and punishment. I could have run from Him, unwilling to humble myself or unwilling to acknowledge the sting that I was wrong. I could have confused my mistake with my identity, thinking, *This means I'm a bad person.* Instead, I acknowledged that I was wrong and offered my heart to God in prayer, asking God to change me. He is a good Father, and His forgiveness is swift — already determined at the cross.

Throughout Scripture, God's rebuke of His children was always an invitation to relationship. From the very beginning when the first man and woman ate the fruit, God has lovingly disciplined His people for our benefit and to accomplish His plan of salvation in the earth.

God is not interested in crushing us. His heart is to save us. If that were not true, then He would not have sent Jesus to do what He did. We can take joy in our relationship with God, even when He corrects us. We should be happy when God speaks to us and speaks to us clearly. We should rejoice that His correction is a form of love. When we receive it that way, we can experience it as God's embrace and kindness to us. We receive love and transformation, and we decrease our chances of needing discipline again because we now understand.

When God corrects you, let it touch the depths of you. Allow yourself to feel deeply, and don't be quick to escape the correction. Let His voice penetrate to the roots of rebellion and independence in your heart, and trust that His correction is an expression of love. He is maturing you into the image of Jesus. He knows your potential. Receive God's correction as love today.

Prayer Starter:

- ❑ Thank God for His love and that He corrects us as a loving Father.
- ❑ Ask God if there is any area in your heart or life that He wants to correct.
- ❑ Ask God to help you receive and give correction well.

Journal Experience:

What have your past experiences taught you about correction (specifically correction from earthly authorities like parents, pastors, teachers, and so forth)? Do you have mostly good or bad examples of discipline and correction in your life? Ask God what He wants to say about the bad ones?

_____

_____

_____

_____

_____

_____

_____

_____

_____

_____

_____

_____

_____

_____

_____

_____

_____

_____

_____

_____

_____

_____

Action Step:

Choose a Christian friend (ideally several of them) and tell them that you want to be more like Jesus every day. Verbally give them ongoing permission to alert you to anything in your life that poorly represents Him. Ask them to lovingly confront you whenever you're out of step with Him and also to encourage you when you're letting Him shine.

Supplemental Reading:
- ❑ 2 Samuel 12:1-15
- ❑ John 21

DAY 30
LETTING GOD FATHER YOU

James Loruss (with Art Thomas)

A lot of my listening is God the Father fathering me in ways that my earthly father was not able to father me.
~ Rusty Rustenbach

> **Isaiah 64:8** — Yet you, Lord, are our Father. We are the clay, You are the Potter; we are all the work of Your hand. (NIV)

FOR MANY PEOPLE THE WORD "FATHER" CAN BE A touchy subject. Many have been deeply wounded — abused, neglected, and/or abandoned — by their earthly fathers. This skews our perspective of "fatherhood" and typically causes us to misunderstand who God really is. Many of us assume God is just like the dad we grew up with.

No matter how bad or how good your earthly dad has treated you, it doesn't change God's nature and love for you. He is a good Dad. He's the best Dad. And He loves you more than even the best earthly father could ever dream.

"But God demonstrates His own love for us in this: While we were still sinners, Christ died for us" (Romans 5:8). God is not waiting for you to "get your act together." He is not withholding His presence from you until you become a better person. In fact, there is no possible way to truly become a better person without His presence. The Christian life only happens when we trust God to do all the work in us Himself.

God does, however, see your potential. Even when all mankind was dead in our sin, Jesus considered you worth dying for. God knows that if you step into your full potential in Him, the kingdom of darkness will be wrecked. Sons of God — partnered with Jesus — destroy the devil's work. (See 1 John 3:8 and John 20:21.)

God loves the world so much that He sent His Son to set them free (John 3:16-17). Then, in His love for us, the Father chose to partner with us the same way He partnered with Jesus. (See John 5:19 and 15:5.) He surrendered the fulfillment of His greatest desire (the salvation of all mankind) to the context of partnership with us. "For God so loved the world that He gave His one and only Son..." But then Jesus delegated His commission to us: "As the Father has sent Me, I am sending you." In other words, God loves the world so much that He also sent us!

This is why it's so important that we let God father us. He wants to shape us into full expressions of sonship. Romans 8:29 says that God's plan from the beginning was for us "to be conformed to the image of His Son, that He [Jesus] might be the firstborn among many brothers and sisters." Jesus was the prototype of sonship, showing us what it looks like when a human being lives free from sin, in right relationship with the Father. And then He paid the price with His own blood so that we too could be free from sin, in right relationship with the Father.

God's greatest desire is to see His nature perfectly displayed in you. He has called you to be set apart for His purposes. The reason God wants to Father us is so we'll ultimately look like Him. He says, "Be holy for I am holy" (1 Peter 1:16).

In John 8:31-47, Jesus makes the case that we are children of whomever we act like. In verse 39, He argues, "If you were Abraham's children...then you would do what Abraham did." And in verse 42, He continues, "If God were your Father, you would love Me..." Instead, He points out that their desire to murder and their lying tongues prove that they are children of the devil, doing what the devil does (John 8:44).

Salvation is a transfer of fatherhood. We are adopted as God's sons and given the Spirit of sonship (Romans 8:15). God's Holy Spirit takes up residence in our hearts and begins working to fully accomplish the Father's plan, making us like Him (Philippians 2:13).

The reason God wants to make you more like Jesus is not because He doesn't love you the way you are. He loved you when you were still dead in sin! The reason God wants to make you more like Jesus is because He knows your potential. He knows who you were created to be. It's not that He doesn't love you the way you are; it's that He loves you enough to help you become the beautiful, glorious expression of

His heart that you were always supposed to be.

Let God father you. Let Him encourage your heart even when you don't think you deserve it. Let Him confront your pride and independence even when it makes you uncomfortable or frustrated. Let Him expose sin in your life and challenge you to live differently with His help. And let Him live His life through you so that others around you can encounter Him.

"Yet to all who did receive Him, to those who believed in His name, He gave the right to become children of God" (John 1:12).

Prayer Starter:

- ❏ Thank God for being the best Father.
- ❏ Ask God if you've been holding any offense against Him because of experiences with your earthly father figures. Ask for His love and correction.
- ❏ Ask the Holy Spirit to partner with you today to reveal God's heart to someone as Father.

Journal Experience:

Today's journal exercise is a little long, but it's an important one. Ask Father God if there has been anything you have been believing about Him that isn't true. Write down the first thing that comes to mind. If the thing that comes to mind is something you don't technically believe in intellectually, write it down anyway. You may find that your heart has led you to live contrary to your theology, and the Father is showing you that you aren't actually living as though what you believe is true.

_____

_____

_____

Second, ask Him, "Father, what truth do You want me to know about You?"

_____

_____

_____

_____

Next, pray, "I choose to forgive my earthly father for any way He conveyed to me the lie that...

(_fill in the blank..._)_____

_____

_____

Now pray, "Father, I give to You this lie that I have believed. What do You want to give me in return?" Write down whatever comes to mind. It may be words, a picture, or some other feeling. If it's symbolic, first write the symbol and then your interpretation of what it might mean. Again, go with the first thing that comes to you.

_____

_____

_____

_____

_____

Now ask Him, "Father, what do You think of me?" Write down the thoughts that come to mind.

_____

_____

_____

_____

_____

_____

_____

_____

_____

Finally, ask Him, "Father, what do you think of my earthly dad and the way he treated me?" Write down the thoughts that come to mind.

_____

_____

_____

_____

_____

_____

_____

_____

_____

_____

_____

_____

_____

_____

_____

_____

_____

_____

_____

Action Step:

Today's action step will be different for everyone:

If you have a strained relationship with your earthly father, he is still living, and you have a way to contact him: Contact your earthly dad — preferably in person if possible — and try to reconcile (or if full reconciliation isn't yet possible, at least make the following steps in that direction). If he knows you've been angry at him, verbally forgive him. If you said or did hurtful things to him, verbally apologize.

If you have a healthy relationship with your earthly father, he is still living, and you have a way to contact him: Contact your earthly dad — preferrably in person if possible — or write a letter to him. Speak words of encouragement to him. Tell him about things that really meant a lot to you growing up, and thank him for raising you to be who you are today.

If your earthly father is no longer living or if you have no way of contacting him: Do one of the above activities for a father-figure in your life — perhaps a pastor, another family member, or a close family friend who has cared for you and spoken into your life in some way.

Supplemental Reading:
☐   Matthew 7:7-12
☐   John 8:31-47
☐   Romans

SECTION 7:
Maturing in Prophetic Ministry

DAY 31
MAKE LOVE YOUR HIGHEST AIM

Jonathan Ammon

When you're comfortable with love, you're comfortable with God because "God is love" (1 John 4:16).

~ *Leif Hetland*

> **1 Corinthians 13:2** — If I have the gift of prophecy and can fathom all mysteries and all knowledge, and if I have a faith that can move mountains, but do not have love, I am nothing. (NIV)

> **1 John 4:7-8** — Dear friends, let us love one another, for love comes from God. Everyone who loves has been born of God and knows God. Whoever does not love does not know God, because God is love. (NIV)

PAUL WROTE TO THE CORINTHIANS TO ENCOURAGE them to focus their zeal for spiritual gifts on edifying and building up others. (See 1 Corinthians 12-14.) One of the most beautiful passages ever written on love comes in the middle of a discussion of spiritual gifts and hearing God for others. Paul emphatically teaches that love should be the goal, and that love never fails (1 Corinthians 13:8).

When we minister in the supernatural, when we pray for miracles, when we listen to God for others, and when we seek revelation, the goal is love. The purpose is to love people with the gifts that God gives. Prophecy is meant to serve others and to pour God's love into their lives. We are to love others with prophecy. The gift is not for us.

We can be tempted to desire prophecy so that we can minister more effectively, be more successful, fulfill our callings, gain respect and accolades, or feel good about ourselves. But prophecy is not about us. It is about God and His love for the person in front of us. It is about what they need and about what God wants to say to them. It is about communicating God's heart and love in a specific supernatural way that will bless someone.

We are told to pursue love and to eagerly desire spiritual gifts (1 Corinthians 14:1). We are to go after love. We are to pursue the heart and character of God. We are to desire God's love to pour out of our lives, and we are told to desire to prophesy.

We are commanded to desire God to pour out His love through His words. We are commanded to desire to love people through prophecy. We are commanded to desire to see people reconciled to God through prophecy. We are commanded to desire to see people pulled from the brink of despair through prophecy. We are commanded to desire to demonstrate God's love through prophecy.

The goal and the aim of all of this is love. We can prophesy accurately over hundreds, but if we don't have love we will be nothing. Our ministry may be successful. We may have a great reputation, and God may work through us, but our own lives will be hollow and empty. Love will not have it's way because our motives are not in line with God's.

We may prophesy inaccurately. We may make mistakes. But if love is our genuine goal and aim, we cannot fail. God's grace covers our failure and weakness, and the love that He has worked in our lives will bear fruit.

When seeking to hear God's voice for others, don't focus on what will impress. Focus on how to love someone with prophecy. Ask God to embrace them with His word. Ask God to pour His love out through you. Love never fails.

Prayer Starter:

❑ Thank God for His love for you. Thank Him that He loved you when you were in sin and that He has been patient and gracious to you.
❑ Ask God to examine the motivations of your heart, Tell Him you want to love and serve others with prophecy.
❑ Ask God for opportunities to love others with prophecy and hearing His voice this week.

Journal Experience:

What are some unhealthy or "negative" motivations that might make people want to prophesy?

_____

_____

_____

_____

_____

_____

_____

_____

_____

What are some healthy or "positive" motivations that might make people want to prophesy?

_____

_____

_____

_____

_____

_____

_____

_____

_____

List three names of people you know (and with whom you regularly interact) who you feel are in desperate need of experiencing God's love.

_____

_____

_____

Action Step:

Look at the three names you just wrote down. Ask the Lord if there is a specific way He would like to love those people through you.

You may want to journal what the Lord tells you and then how the experience went:

_____

_____

_____

_____

_____

_____

_____

_____

_____

_____

_____

_____

_____

_____

_____

_____

_____

_____

_____

_____

_____

_____

_____

_____

_____

_____

_____

_____

_____

_____

_____

_____

_____

Supplemental Reading:
- ❑ 1 Corinthians 13
- ❑ 1 John 4

Day 32
Practice in the Context of Community

James Loruss (with Art Thomas)

I need fellowship. I need people checking me. I need to be in relationship with other people. There's no such thing as anyone hearing accurately from God off alone. You don't do that. God didn't set it up like that.

~ *R. Loren Sandford*

Acts 13:1 — Now in the church at Antioch there were prophets and teachers: Barnabas, Simeon called Niger, Lucius of Cyrene, Manaen (who had been brought up with Herod the tetrarch) and Saul. (NIV)

Acts 15:32 — Judas and Silas, who themselves were prophets, said much to encourage and strengthen the believers. (NIV)

1 Corinthians 14:24-25 — But if an unbeliever or an inquirer comes in while

> everyone is prophesying, they are convicted of sin and are brought under judgment by all, as the secrets of their hearts are laid bare. So they will fall down and worship God, exclaiming, "God is really among you!" (NIV)

BEFORE JESUS CAME, PROPHETS WERE RELATIVELY rare. Even during times when large groups of prophets are mentioned in the Old Testament, usually only one stands out as the one God is truly using. Only on a few occasions do we see many people prophesying accurately. Often the biblical prophets were lonely ministers who spoke as the sole representative of God's voice to mankind.

But now that Jesus has come — now that we who follow Him have been transformed by the indwelling Holy Spirit — those who speak for God do so from within a spiritual and prophetic family. Acts 13:1 says, "There were certain prophets," and it identifies that they were "*in* the church." No longer does the word "prophet" carry the connotation of "outsider." All of us — prophets and prophetic people alike — are one family in Christ, and we all need each other.

Far too many prophetic people have taken pride in their loneliness. There's a difference between being ostracized by an obstinate people who hate you (as happened to the Old Testament prophets) and avoiding community due to fear of rejection or a need to be "unique." You cannot love the voice of God without loving the Word of God, Jesus. And you cannot love the Word of God without loving His Body, the Church. True New Testament prophetic people run toward the community of faith, not away from it.

New Testament prophecy always comes from within the context of the Christian community called "the Church." While prophetic words can certainly happen outside of church meetings, they always come from people who are part of Christ's Body.

The most common form of prophetic ministry that we read about in the New Testament happens inside church gatherings. That's because (1) God loves to speak to His kids, (2) we need encouragement from Him to remind us who we are and to propel us into the mission field, and (3) it's the safest environment for learning. A healthy church provides an atmosphere of love that gently corrects and faithfully covers mistakes when they are made.

This aspect of practice is important. It would be silly if a professional athlete only practiced on game days. They are the best because they live and breathe their sport, and they practice frequently with their own team. Christians can learn from this. The best place to learn to prophesy is with people who aren't hostile to us. It's a lot easier to give a prophetic word in a room full of grace-filled Christians than it is to total strangers on the streets.

Besides that, Paul says if an unbeliever walks into a church meeting where everyone is prophesying, he will fall down and worship God (1 Corinthians 14:24-25). Many times I've seen hearts softened and lives transformed as a small group of Christians took time to prophesy over each other in a meeting. Clearly, the most successfully evangelistic church meetings are the ones where a prophetic people love well and represent Jesus with their words, actions, and spiritual gifts.

Admittedly, the church Paul addressed in

Corinth gathered in homes. It would be a logistical nightmare to try facilitating everyone prophesying in our typical, large American churches. Generally speaking, the best setting in which to implement this sort of community setting is still a home group. I highly recommend either joining or starting a small group where everyone is encouraged to study Scripture, hear from God, and share with the rest of the group. Big meetings are still great, but they serve a different purpose.

Learning how to better share a word from God should be a normal part of discipleship. If we all practice in the context of community, then mature believers can model appropriate etiquette and behavior, and new believers can be immersed in a safe environment where hearing from God and judging revelation are understood as "normal." Take time to practice in fellowship with other believers.

Prayer Starter:

- ❑ Thank God for saving you into a spiritual family. Praise Him for His wisdom in designing the Church to function this way.
- ❑ Ask God to make you the type of person who is safe for others to practice around. Ask Him to make you more loving and gracious than you've ever been.
- ❑ Pray for your church or small group to be a spiritual family where spiritual gifts can be learned, developed, and encouraged more effectively than they are now.

Journal Experience:

Ask God why He considered it important to design the Church as a family. Write down what comes to mind.

_____

_____

_____

_____

_____

_____

_____

_____

_____

_____

_____

_____

_____

_____

_____

_____

_____

_____

_____

_____

_____

_____

_____

_____

_____

_____

_____

_____

_____

_____

Action Step:

Find three Christians to encourage today. Ask the Lord beforehand to speak through you and to make the interaction natural. What you share with the person does not need to be "prophetic" in the typical sense unless God specifically gives you something. What you say may just be an encouraging thought from your own heart. Look the person in the eye as you talk to them, and ask them at the end if what you said made sense.

Supplemental Reading:
❑   1 Corinthians 14:1-25

DAY 33
MAINTAINING HUMILITY AND HUMANITY

James Loruss (with Art Thomas)

God is scouring the earth for people who He can trust. Please… Because if He can trust us in our faithfulness – if He can trust us in our innocence – He will reveal His secrets to us.

~ R. Loren Sandford

> **Romans 12:3** — For by the grace given me I say to every one of you: Do not think of yourself more highly than you ought, but rather think of yourself with sober judgment, in accordance with the faith God has distributed to each of you. (NIV)
>
> **Luke 2:52** — And Jesus grew in wisdom and stature, and in favor with God and man. (NIV)

WHEN I FIRST STARTED GROWING IN THE PROPHETIC, I made a good number of mistakes. During the making of our first movie, *Paid in Full*, Art and I had just returned from filming at a place where the entire church culture was prophetic—everyone around us was always sharing something from the Lord. It wasn't my first experience with the prophetic. Many times I had heard from God for others, but my prior experience was nothing like this place where almost every Christian I met was sharing what they were hearing from God, multiple times a day.

It rubbed off. I came home so excited to share God's heart with others. I wanted to declare what He was speaking with everyone I talked to. I went from not really sharing at all to sharing with everyone.

The excitement was good—don't get me wrong! More of us need this sort of zeal for the prophetic. The Bible says to "be eager to prophesy" (1 Corinthians 14:39).

But the Bible also says, "It is fine to be zealous, provided the purpose is good" (Galatians 4:18). The problem was that I quickly became more excited about me being able to give someone a word from God than I was for God to love that person. It became more about my own ability to hear Him than about Him being heard.

The Lord gently corrected me, showing me that I was more interested in seeing how many people I could prophesy over than how many I could love. He put my focus back on Him and His love. It's amazing how quickly our motives get twisted when our gaze is not set on Jesus.

When our focus turns in a selfish direction, it's easy for our prophetic experiences to become more important than the people God has given us for relationship. Anytime we find ourselves more fascinated by our prophetic words and experiences than we are with building one another up, we have disconnected from Jesus and are no longer walking in union with Him. Colossians 2:18-19 warns us, "Do not let anyone who delights in false humility and the worship of angels disqualify you. Such a person also goes into great detail about what they have seen; they are puffed up with idle notions by their unspiritual mind. They have lost connection with the Head [Jesus]…"

There's nothing wrong with seeing angels. Such occurrences were common throughout the New Testament. The problem isn't even with talking about our prophetic encounters. The New Testament writers did that too. And the problem isn't technically about sharing the details either (otherwise John would have been in sin for going into so much detail in the book of Revelation). The problem is when prophetic experiences become more important to us than love, service, faithfulness, humility, and building others up.

Far too many prophetic people have allowed insecurity to lead them. They put on a false persona of "super-spirituality" that is supposed to make other people think more highly of them. They act as though they have special insight into the spiritual realm that makes them some sort of heavenly "insider."

Unfortunately, these masks are sometimes so convincing that others play along in order to get close to the super-spiritual person, thinking that he or she has some sort of hidden knowledge or access to God that they don't. They gather a group of sycophants, suck-ups, and flatterers around them to make themselves feel validated and to hide their fragile egos from anyone who would challenge their so-called "gift" or revelations.

How did people who once loved Jesus "lose connection with the Head?" How could people who started out well drift so far from Him?

It usually doesn't happen overnight. It usually happens with small compromises. Perhaps it starts with legitimate encounters with God that we tell some friends about. They're amazed, and it makes us feel important, popular, or unique to have heard God in such a way. But then the encounters stop for some reason, and when people come back to hear more, we feel a need to perform. Maybe we don't want to let them down. Maybe we don't want them to think we sinned. Maybe we want to feel again the thrill of the attention we once had. Whatever the reason, we either make something up or begin listening to whatever spirit will tell us what we want to hear. This is how pride leads us so quickly into destruction.

The simple solution is to deliberately maintain your humanity. Whenever people start putting you on a pedestal, remind them that you're just like them. Spend more time asking others about their experiences and celebrating them than you do your own. Be down-to-earth. Engage in real relationships. Confess to fellow Christians when you mess up.

Have fun! Play a board game or throw a Frisbee with people. Go for a hike with someone or enjoy dinner with friends. In short, do something that doesn't have to be "spiritualized." It will be good for your emotional and spiritual health, and it will help the people around you to relate to you and feel loved.

"And Jesus grew in wisdom and stature, and

in favor with God and man" (Luke 2:52). To be Christ-like is to be a well-rounded human being. The more like Him we become, the more we will value and engage in human relationships. Yes, some will reject us (technically rejecting Him in us), but many will be drawn to His presence in us. We will have favor both with God and with other people.

Be relational. Honor others above yourself. Live an authentic and transparent life as you grow in Jesus. Remain part of the Body of Christ. Remain connected to the Head. Prioritize love and union with Him.

Prayer Starter:

- ❏ Thank Jesus for demonstrating through His earthly life what it looks like to be "fully human in every way" (Hebrews 2:17).
- ❏ Ask the Holy Spirit if there is any hint of pride or a need to perform in your heart that might lead to destruction.
- ❏ Ask the Lord to help you fully engage in healthy relationships and to love others well.

Journal Experience:

Ask the Lord what spiritual and emotional pitfalls He knows you need to be most cautious of when it comes to prophetic ministry. Write them down.

_____

_____

_____

_____

_____

_____

_____

_____

_____

_____

_____

_____

_____

_____

_____

Action Step:

Do something fun with one or more fellow believers. If spiritual conversation comes up, that's fine, but don't try to make that happen. Make your goal to simply enjoy each other's company.

Supplemental Reading:
❏ Appendix B: Staying Real and Grounded.

Day 34
Teach Others to Discern God's Voice

Jonathan Ammon

Every saint can be taught how to hear the voice of God. And they can learn to listen, hear, obey, and be a voice for God.

~ *Bill Hamon*

> **2 Timothy 2:2** — And the things you have heard me say in the presence of many witnesses entrust to reliable people who will also be qualified to teach others. (NIV)

GOD'S VISION FOR THE WORLD IS THE multiplication of His glory through love-relationships with His children. This includes hearing His voice and knowing His love.

We have a part to play in that multiplication. We must pass on what we have heard and learned. What God has sown into our lives we must sow into the lives of others. What God has invested in us we must invest in others.

As we learn to hear God's voice, we have the responsibility of helping others tune their ears to the call of the Father. This may be evangelism, discipleship, church planting, equipping, or many other kinds of ministry. God's voice and word must saturate all that we do.

Teaching others to discern God's voice is a process of love and discovery. You cannot hear for them. You cannot be their ears; you must equip them to hear for themselves.

For all of us, this begins with salvation and continues with the sure and reliable prophetic word of the Scripture. God will speak to us in many ways right from the beginning of our relationship with Him. Paul started His relationship with Jesus with a vision and a prophetic word from Ananias. God does not limit the ways He speaks to us because of our level of maturity. However, our ability to handle and discern revelation correctly will unquestionably grow (and grow healthily) when we discern God's voice in His word.

When coaching new believers to hear God's voice, I always begin with the Scripture. I work with many people who come out of different religious backgrounds. Their view of God must be transformed. They hear and see through the lens of a lifetime of false religion, and the sure, reliable Word of Scripture is always the safest place to start.

Scripture familiarizes us with God's voice and His character. It guides us into an experience with Him and keeps us safe as we seek that experience. Scripture is the revelation by which we measure all other revelation and is the objective basis for our discernment.

Jesus instructed us to make disciples and to "teach them to obey all that I have commanded you" (Matthew 28:18-20). This does not mean teaching a list of commands. This means teaching the action and heart attitude of obedience. That way, whether it is a plain command in Scripture or a specific command from the Holy Spirit, we will be ready to obey.

I often start new believers with Christ's commands in Scripture. They immediately know that God wants them to share the Good News with their friends and family (Mark 5:20). They hear God's voice in Scripture. Then I ask them to silently pray and ask God who He specifically wants them to share with that week. They know that God's will is for them to share the Good News, and they are asking God for specific direction within that obedience. This is a safe place to hear God's direction, and the fact that it is a biblical mandate on God's heart provides immediate faith that God will answer. Everyone I've worked with has found it easy to hear God like this.

As we familiarize ourselves with God's voice in this way, we learn to listen in other ways. We listen for what God thinks about us. We listen for God's direction in more general areas of our lives. We listen for God's encouragement for others. We do all of this in the context of community and Scripture.

Faith grows as we continue to step out and as we continue to hear God's love and direction on a regular basis. We learn to humble ourselves and submit to the community's testing of what we hear, and we learn to align what we hear with Scripture.

This process takes time, but there are simple ways to begin immediately. I often ask people, "What is God teaching you?" God can teach through

Scripture, a sermon, experiences, etc. Regardless of the form of communication, it is indeed communication and therefore an expression of His voice. When they respond with what God has been teaching them, I ask "What are you going to do about that?" This encourages a response to God's voice, and as we respond to what God speaks we step into greater revelation. We become good stewards of His voice.

If someone responds, "I don't know what God is teaching me," we then have an opportunity to encourage them to listen to the voice of God and to offer our help in equipping them to hear God's Word. In short, we point people to the Scriptures first and then teach them to ask the right questions and obey.

Prayer Starter:

- ❑ Thank God for teaching you by His Spirit. Thank Him for the people He has placed in your life that have taught you to hear His voice.
- ❑ Ask God for wisdom and discernment in teaching others.
- ❑ Ask God for the opportunity to help others hear from Him and teach them how to hear God's voice.

Journal Experience:

What are some ways you have been taught to hear God's voice? What were some breakthrough moments in hearing God's voice? How can you use these to teach others?

_____

_____

_____

_____

_____

_____

_____

_____

_____

_____

_____

_____

_____

_____

_____

_____

_____

_____

_____

_____

_____

_____

_____

_____

_____

_____

_____

_____

_____

_____

_____

Action Step:

This week ask someone, "What is God teaching you lately?" Then (assuming they have an answer) follow up with, "What are you going to do about that?"

After they have shared, share about what and how God has been speaking to you. See where the conversation goes.

Supplemental Reading:
- ❑ Matthew 28:18-20
- ❑ Ephesians 4:1-11

DAY 35
OBEY GOD WITHOUT HESITATION

James Loruss

Everything that we have is because of Jesus' obedience. My obedience allows me to participate in what Jesus' obedience bought and paid for.

~ Joe Funaro

Matthew 7:24-27 — Therefore everyone who hears these words of Mine and puts them into practice is like a wise man who built his house on the rock. The rain came down, the streams rose, and the winds blew and beat against that house; yet it did not fall, because it had its foundation on the rock. But everyone who hears these words of Mine and does not put them into practice is like a foolish man who built his house on sand. The rain came down, the streams rose, and the winds blew and beat against that house, and it fell with a great crash." (NIV)

> **Luke 11:28** — He replied, "Blessed rather are those who hear the word of God and obey it." (NIV)

> **James 1:22** — Do not merely listen to the word, and so deceive yourselves. Do what it says. (NIV)

AS YOU JUST READ, THERE IS A BLESSING FOR THOSE who not only hear God's word but then obey it as well. It amazes me when Christians equate hearing a message with living the Christian life. Week after week they attend a sermon and think that this is Christianity. But hearing God's words is not the same as obeying what He says.

Let's take the twelve disciples for example. Jesus said, "Follow Me." The disciples heard Jesus invite them into discipleship, but merely hearing Jesus speak did not make Him Lord over their lives. The same goes for us.

The parable you read from Matthew 7 compares two builders who were building houses: one built on the sand and the other on the rock. I think we all know where this story is heading. If we continue reading we see that the man who built his house on the rock was the only one whose house was firmly planted. Notice that both men heard the words of Jesus. The difference here is neither in the men nor the message. The only difference was whether or not they put it into practice.

Both men were builders, so they both had the capability to build. Both men had ears, and both heard the word. The difference was their foundation. Your foundation is not in Christ if you're not choosing to obey what He says. James 2:18 says, "...Show me your faith without deeds, and I will show you my faith by my deeds."

Your deeds are evidence of your faith in God. If someone never obeys what God says, then they're not really a disciple of Christ, are they? The key is obedience. Merely hearing Jesus doesn't make Him Lord of your life. The Pharisees heard Jesus and even knew the Scriptures, but they still crucified Him. We need to be careful we don't become those who know the Scriptures but never let the Spirit who inspired those words transform our hearts, minds, and actions.

Often when people tell me they don't hear God speaking anymore or they're frustrated that He's not telling them anything different, I ask them, "What's the last thing you heard Him say?" Then I will ask them if they obeyed. I've found many times in my life that God will choose to not tell me anything else until I walk in complete obedience to the last thing He told me. It doesn't make much sense for God to give you something else to work on when you haven't been obedient with the last thing He told you.

The more we mature in Christ, the more we learn to respond immediately. The more we become like Jesus, the more we are led by the Spirit—not arguing with God or running from His promptings. Jesus said, "The One who sent Me is with Me; He has not left Me alone, for I always do what pleases Him" (John 8:29). Mature, Christ-like children of God "always do what pleases Him."

It's natural when you're starting out to wrestle with the things God is telling you to do. It's even natural to struggle when you've been listening to Him for years, but He tells you something that stretches your faith. You can gauge your maturity in Christ (and therefore your maturity in the prophetic) by the development of immediate obedience. It is the fruit of trust in a faithful and loving Father.

I'm not just talking about the subtle nudges we feel when God wants us to pray for someone or do a good deed. Those things are important, but let's not forget about the commands the Bible already gives. If you're not sure where to start, try the commission Jesus gave us all: "Go and make disciples of all nations…" (Matthew 28:19). It's the only commission Jesus gave us.

My friend Art says, "Every command Jesus ever gave is impossible to do apart from union with Him. Jesus said in John 15:5, 'Apart from Me you can do nothing.' Therefore every command of Jesus is an invitation into relationship." God never intends for you to obey Him purely in your own strength. When God gives a command, He expects us to say "yes" to partnership with Him. And when we do, He responds immediately with the grace to obey.

Prayer Starter:

- ❑ Thank Jesus for setting an example of perfect obedience.
- ❑ Ask God if there is any area of your life where you have not been obedient to His voice.
- ❑ Ask God to help you be more frequently obedient to share the Gospel with people. Ask the Holy Spirit to give you an opportunity today.

Journal Experience:

Write down the last thing you heard God ask you to do. If you can't remember, ask Him right now for something. Next, ask Him what manageable steps you will need to make to accomplish what He's asked you to do. Write those down too.

_____

_____

_____

_____

_____

_____

_____

_____

_____

_____

_____

_____

_____

_____

_____

_____

_____

_____

_____

_____

_____

_____

_____

_____

_____

_____

_____

_____

_____

_____

_____

_____

_____

_____

_____

_____

_____

Action Step:

Take action! Try and do at least one step from the list you made above.

Supplemental Reading:
❏   Hebrews 11

SECTION 8:
God's Voice in Ministry

DAY 36
GOD'S VOICE IN EVANGELISM

Jonathan Ammon

I don't wait for the Lord to say, "Go;" I wait for the Lord to say, "No." And that's very, very seldom.

~ *Joe Funaro*

Acts 16:6-10 — Paul and his companions traveled throughout the region of Phrygia and Galatia, having been kept by the Holy Spirit from preaching the word in the province of Asia. When they came to the border of Mysia, they tried to enter Bithynia, but the Spirit of Jesus would not allow them to. So they passed by Mysia and went down to Troas. During the night Paul had a vision of a man of Macedonia standing and begging him, "Come over to Macedonia and help us." After Paul had seen the vision, we got ready at once to leave for Macedonia, concluding that God had called us to preach the gospel to them. (NIV)

JESUS CAME "TO SEEK AND TO SAVE THAT WHICH was lost" (Luke 19:10), and making disciples out of this lost and dying world remains what God is most interested in. God's voice calls out to the orphan and invites them into the family. God's Spirit works through us as we go into the highways and byways and compel people to come to the marriage supper of the Lamb (Luke 14:23; Revelation 19:9).

When we focus on reaching the lost we often find God's voice easier to hear because we step into His heart for His creation. We step into His priorities and His interests. I've had God give words of knowledge that resulted in salvation. I've conveyed prophecy that brought people who had never known Him to the throne. I've seen God give names, house numbers, and street locations. I've seen the Holy Spirit give visions of specific people, places, and prayer needs. God will go to great lengths to reach the lost, and He will use us if we are willing to listen.

God has already commanded us and directed us to "Go." He told us to go to the lost. He ordered us to "make disciples." He does not need to tell us again. God's voice may not give us further direction until we go out and obey His standing orders.

Paul and His companions obeyed God's simple direction to "go into all the world" and were following through on a plan to do just that. As they were already in action obeying God, they received direction of where to go and what to do (Acts 16:6-10). God directed them where not to go and where to go. As you go out and obey Jesus' commission, expect and allow God to interrupt, lead, and guide.

Even when we don't listen, evangelism

results in supernatural encounters because the Holy Spirit is desperate to involve Himself in our obedience. But if we do listen—if we pause and ask God to speak—He will give us revelation.

There are so many ways to listen to God as we preach the gospel, and most of them involve listening. God promises, "Call to Me and I will answer you, and will tell you great and hidden things that you have not known" (Jeremiah 33:3). We have a promise that when we ask, God will answer. As we go out to evangelize we can ask, "Where should we go? Who will we meet? What should we say? What should we look for? What does this person need? What do You want to say to this person? Where have You been in this person's life?" God will answer in miraculous ways.

All evangelism is a shared experience with the voice of God. Not only is God speaking to you, but He is speaking to the person you're speaking to—both through your mouth and in their hearts, directly drawing them to Jesus. Whenever we share the Gospel, we are creating opportunities for others to hear God for themselves. In this way, all evangelism is a prophetic encounter.

We have to remember that prophecy is the testimony of Jesus, but our prophetic words and words of knowledge are not the gospel. The Gospel itself is God's prophetic word to the world. It's what He wants proclaimed to all nations. You don't need a crazy testimony of a word of knowledge or a prophetic word. You need to proclaim the Good News that Jesus Christ died on the cross for the forgiveness of sins and rose from the dead so that all could have a new life with Him in the Kingdom of God. He is Lord of all. This gospel must be preached to all nations, and it is this gospel that is the power to save.

The Holy Spirit confirms the Gospel with signs and wonders. This means He works with our Gospel proclamation to confirm our words. If we go and preach the Gospel, the Holy Spirit is guaranteed to show up. Go and preach the Gospel. As you go, never stop listening to God. Never stop asking God questions. Never stop asking God for help. Listen to the Lord and say what He says to His Creation.

Prayer Starter:

- ❑ Thank God for His constant pursuit of the lost. Ask Him to give you His heart and to hear His call to those who don't know Him.
- ❑ Ask God for boldness and compassion.
- ❑ Ask God for divine appointments this week. Ask Him for specific words and prophetic experiences with the lost.

Journal Experience:

If you could express God's heart to a lost person and they would listen to whatever you said, what would you say?

_____

_____

_____

_____

_____

_____

_____

_____

_____

_____

_____

_____

_____

_____

_____

_____

_____

Action Step:

The following Action Step is inspired by and adapted from Kevin Dedmon's *The Ultimate Treasure Hunt*. **Blank "Treasure Hunt" sheets with instructions can be downloaded for free under the "Other" / "Downloads" tab at www.SupernaturalTruth.com.**

STEP 1: Read Acts 9:10-19. Notice that an "ordinary" disciple received a vision from the Lord and was told what street to go to, the house on the street to go to, the name of the man he was to pray for, and what the man needed prayer for.

STEP 2: On a blank sheet of paper, list the following categories with plenty of room to write down "clues" (or things that the Lord tells you to look for as you search for His lost treasure) under each category:

- ❖ Locations:
- ❖ Names:
- ❖ Appearance of the Person:
- ❖ Prayer Needs:
- ❖ Unusual:

STEP 3: Flip the paper over. You are not asking the Lord to give you clues for categories. You are asking the Lord to give you clues for people. Listen to the Lord with an open ear to hear anything.

STEP 4: Take five minutes and ask the Lord for "clues" or words of knowledge. Write down everything, unfiltered and unsorted on the back of the paper.

STEP 5: Sort the clues into the categories on the first side of the paper.

STEP 6: If you're doing this activity with a group (which is ideal), have everyone in the group read their clues out loud. Do not write down anyone else's clues on your paper. You will have to pay attention to your own. But keep other people's clues in mind as you are out to help them find theirs.

STEP 7: Decide how large of a group you are taking. If you have too many locations for one group to reach, split up. I usually take a larger group and send people off in pairs when they find clues. A group of ten will walk together, one person will say, "Look a man in a red hat! Didn't you write that down?" "Wow, yes I did!" Then those two will go together to talk to the man in the red hat. The whole group approaching one person is intimidating.

STEP 8: Prayerfully use a map (perhaps on a Smartphone if available) to make a plan or route to reach the locations God gave you.

STEP 9: Decide how you are going to approach people. (i.e. "Hi, we are on a treasure hunt, and you are on our list." "Hello, I was praying today, and God told me to pray for someone who had ____. Can I pray for you?" "Hello, we are out praying for people today. Would you like prayer for anything?") Remember to be Spirit-led. Remember the person. Do unto others as you would have them do unto you.

STEP 10: Pray and Go! Be bold, for the Lord your God is with you!

DAY 37
GOD'S VOICE IN DISCIPLESHIP

Jonathan Ammon

It's so simple, but because our culture is so crazy busy — with iPhones, and Twitter, and Facebook, and all the stuff that we do — people aren't hearing God's voice. Therefore they go to their pastor or they go to a church leader, and they don't know what God's will is for their life. You know, if they came to me for guidance or direction, I'd say, "When's the last time you locked up yourself in prayer for a couple hours until you heard God's voice?" Most people haven't done that for 30 minutes!

~ *Paul Maurer*

> **Matthew 28:19-20** — Therefore go and make disciples of all nations, baptizing them in the name of the Father and of the Son and of the Holy Spirit, and teaching them to obey everything I have commanded you. And surely I am with you always, to the very end of the age. (NIV)

THE GREAT COMMISSION COMMANDS US TO MAKE disciples. We are to teach them to obey Christ and all that He says. In order to obey we must hear. In order to follow Christ we must see where He is going. We have to hear His word and understand it so that we can bear fruit (Matthew 13:23).

Jesus said, "A disciple is not above his teacher, but everyone when he is fully trained will be like his teacher." The prophetic end-vision for discipleship is Jesus Christ Himself. We are in training to live out the revelation of Jesus Christ. We are and will be like Jesus. We resemble Him when we hear His voice and obey it. We are transformed to be like Him when we see Him as He really is (2 Corinthians 3:18; 1 John 3:2).

Jesus commanded us to go and make disciples "teaching them to obey everything that I have commanded you" (Matthew 28:18-20). As mentioned on Day 34, we aren't to teach everything Jesus commanded but to teach "to obey." The focus is not knowledge but obedience. As disciple-makers it is our job to equip others to hear and obey the voice of God. It is our job to help them see Jesus and allow themselves to be changed into His image and likeness.

While we all have a prophetic responsibility to hear God and reveal Jesus to others, we can't have a relationship with Jesus for other people. They can't live vicariously through us. We make disciples of Jesus, not of ourselves.

We represent and demonstrate Jesus to our fullest ability, but even at our very best they follow Him as they follow us. They must know Him, and hear Him, and see Him for themselves. We must guide them into an ongoing encounter with Jesus and help them know how to grow a healthy relationship and experience with Him. We can speak from the throne of Grace, but we also must point the way to the throne. Those we guide must go there themselves. We can share our discoveries in God's presence, but they must make their own discoveries.

Jesus constantly asked questions to His disciples. He was inviting them to discover the truth for themselves. He didn't tell them everything. He didn't show them everything. Instead, He prompted them to learn in relationship with Him. He asked questions, used stories, and said things that were difficult to understand, in order to draw His disciples into a conversation with Him. He wanted them to draw the truth from Him.

In the same way, we must find ways to draw others to Jesus for answers. We have to ask questions rather than provide pat answers. We have to point to Jesus as the source of victory and freedom. We have to encourage others to listen, test, and obey Christ's word.

There are a vast number of ways to do this. Many have been codified and systematized so that others can apply them well, but the principle is to point to Christ and His Word. We often start listening to God in the Bible, obeying and applying His Word, and then tune our ears to the Holy Spirit as we move forward in grace.

I can't pass along a clear understanding of God's voice to someone, but I can pass on questions that illuminate our need to hear. I ask people things like:

❖ What is God teaching you?
❖ What does God say about that?

❖ What is God speaking to you?
❖ Have you asked God about this?
❖ How have you been experiencing the Holy Spirit lately?
❖ How have you been abiding in Christ?
❖ What is God teaching you from Scripture?
❖ What are you hearing God say in prayer?
❖ What are you going to do about that?
❖ What was the last command God gave you personally?
❖ What is God calling you to do?
❖ What has God said about who you are?
❖ What are promises God has given you?

If we are honest, there are times when we will have to say, "I'm not sure," and go back to God to discover His voice again and again.

Prayer Starter:

❑ Praise God for His plan to multiply His glory throughout the earth by making disciples of all nations.
❑ Ask God for a heart to make disciples, to help others to obey Him, and to stay with people as they grow and develop.
❑ Ask God for people who are open and receptive to learning to obey Jesus. Ask God to develop discipleship relationships in your life.

Journal Experience:

What are a few things you have learned from others about hearing God's voice? How did you learn these things?

_____

_____

_____

_____

_____

_____

_____

_____

_____

_____

_____

_____

_____

_____

_____

_____

_____

_____

_____

_____

_____

_____

_____

_____

_____

_____

_____

_____

_____

_____

_____

_____

_____

Action Step:

Ask someone "How are you abiding in Christ? What does that look like?" Have a conversation about it. Learn from them and let them learn from you if they're interested.

Supplemental Reading:
- ❏ Luke 6:40 and 46-49

DAY 38
GOD'S VOICE IN COUNSELING

Art Thomas

When you start hearing God, love comes with it. His word is love. When you get filled with God's love, you start loving people in a greater dimension – a greater capacity. I don't prophesy just because I want to prophesy. I want to love people. I want to change people's lives. That's what this world needs.

~ *Hector Caban*

> **Isaiah 9:6b** — ...And He will be called Wonderful Counselor, Mighty God, Everlasting Father, Prince of Peace. (NIV)

> **Matthew 5:9** — Blessed are the peacemakers, for they will be called children of God. (NIV)

> **James 1:5** — If any of you lacks wisdom, you should ask God, who gives generously to all without finding fault, and it will be given to you. (NIV)

BROKEN PEOPLE NEED AN ENCOUNTER WITH THE ONE who binds up the brokenhearted (Luke 4:18). Jesus is the "Wonderful Counselor," and we do people a great disservice when we try to usurp His role.

However, many times these troubled people come to us with deep wounds and emotional turmoil. Sometimes they've been so abused and disappointed in life that they're afraid of God or deeply confused about who He is. A simple and trite instruction to "pray about it" is worthless. Many don't even feel like God loves them or cares.

This is where we come in as representatives of Jesus — peacemakers who distribute peace and produce righteousness (James 3:18). We can be the bridge that helps a person approach the God they don't know.

I should note up front that some people need professional counseling, and we should not try to intervene in situations that are beyond our skill set. It is never wrong to refer people to pastors and skilled counselors who have more training and experience than we do. Often this is the best option.

While this lesson will be beneficial to the professional as well, any of us can find ourselves in a situation where a hurting person is crying in our living room, asking for wise advice, or begging for answers to the common philosophical question of "Why?"

"Why did my child die?" "Why did my wife leave me?" "Why isn't God taking care of me?" The list goes on.

These are the moments when we can provide a loving response that shows the love of Christ and introduces people to the merciful Father who grieves right along with them. These are the moments when we can physically provide the hug that Jesus so desperately wants that person to feel.

I once ran into a friend of mine on a Sunday morning when both of us dropped off our children in the church nursery. He hadn't been to our church in a long time, and it was good to see him after so many years. We started to make small talk, and that's when he began venting to me about how distant he felt from God.

In that moment I didn't know what to say. I just looked him in the eye and listened. We sat down on some couches in the hallway of our church, and he proceeded to tell me about the struggle his family was facing and the rejection they had experienced from another church.

Sometimes it's not necessary to say anything at all. In fact, most of the time, people just need someone to listen, and your focused, active listening is in itself a revelation of Jesus. It's hard to convince people that God is listening when we—His representatives—aren't. This is an opportunity to visibly illustrate and reveal the God who hears.

My friend's complaint about life quickly evolved into a complaint about God, wondering why He had allowed all this to happen to them. As he spoke I listened for insight from the Holy Spirit, and He came through.

When my friend finished, we sat quietly for a moment. He said, "You look like you're thinking."

"I am," I answered. "I completely understand where you're coming from. I haven't lived it myself, but I get it. You're not broken."

Sometimes people need to hear that their experience isn't abnormal or crazy. Sometimes they need the reassurance of knowing that their problem is being taken seriously but also isn't overwhelming. Here too, we represent Jesus—the One who takes their problem more seriously than anyone and isn't fearful about it.

A scripture came to my mind: "There is no fear in love. But perfect love drives out fear, because fear has to do with punishment. The one who fears is not made perfect in love." (1 John 4:18). I asked the Lord what to do with what I was hearing, and I felt that this wasn't something He wanted me to share so much as it was something He wanted me to address. *How do you want me to address it, Lord?*

All this happened in a split second—the scripture, my question, and then God's answer: "He needs to know My Fatherly love."

I continued, "It seems to me that your experiences have taught you things about God that aren't true, and I believe you will have all the answers you need if you can see a couple things..."

For the next twenty minutes, I told my friend the Gospel. He was a Christian who grew up in church, so none of this was anything new to him. But I knew that the Gospel is the clearest way to explain the love of the Father. The Gospel is the solution-plan for everything because it points to God's love, our need, God's action, and our transformation through union with Him.

I explained death with Christ (Galatians 2:20), resurrection with Christ (Romans 6:5), and our present place of being seated with Him in the heavenly realms (Ephesians 2:6; Revelation 3:21). I talked about everything Jesus has done and everything He wants to continue to do in partnership with us. I explained the problem of evil in the world, God's solution to evil (Jesus), and God's continued mission against evil (the Church). I showed my friend God's role, and I showed him our role.

And when I was finished, my friend said, "If that's true, number one, it's the greatest news that ever existed. And number two, how has no one ever told me this before?"

I smiled and let my friend know that he has probably heard it before at some point, but this is the first time he was ready to receive it.

"I want that," he said emphatically.

We prayed together. My friend recommitted his life to Jesus. In a matter of twenty minutes, my friend went from being distant from God and depressed to rejoicing in the God who loves him, hearing the Father's voice for the first time in years.

My friend and I missed the church service, but we didn't miss Jesus. As he drove home that day, he explained to his wife all the things I had shared with him. Their entire worldview changed in a day. That was about six years ago, and my friends are still passionate for Jesus today, raising their family well.

I wish every case of counseling had such miraculous and instant results. I also have stories of saying and doing all the right things and still having the person reject Jesus. But I share this story to illustrate the way things can work. I represented Jesus to my friend. I listened intently. With direction from the Holy Spirit, I shared the Gospel with him, even though he had probably heard it a thousand times before. I trusted the Lord to help me explain things in a way that my friend would understand.

In that moment, my friend was in no condition to approach God for himself, so I did it on his behalf. But notice that I didn't do things in a way that would make my friend dependent on me.

Instead I introduced him to the only One on whom he can always depend. The best Christian counseling provides a jumpstart in a person's relationship with God, much like the way jumper cables can revive a dead car battery. We who have our engines running provide the charge. But once our friend's engine has been jumpstarted, we disconnect the cables and let them drive.

Prayer Starter:

- ❑ Thank God for being a better counselor than you. Thank Him for times He's counseled you.
- ❑ Ask Jesus to teach you about His nature as the Wonderful Counselor. Ask Him to express that attribute of Himself through you.
- ❑ Ask God if there is anything you can do better to represent Him to anyone you are mentoring.

Journal Experience:

Think of the most painful situation you've ever experienced in your past. Now imagine you have the opportunity to counsel your younger self. Ask the Lord to show you what He wishes you could have known at the time. Ask Him where He was with you in that moment and what He was doing or saying. Ask Him what He has to say about that experience.

My experience is that this activity can bring real, immediate, and lasting healing to your heart today, so take your time and let the Lord speak into that place of pain. Write down what He shows you.

_____

_____

_____

_____

_____

_____

_____

_____

_____

_____

_____

_____

_____

_____

_____

_____

_____

Action Step:

Ask the Holy Spirit if there's anyone He wants you to tell about what you experienced while journaling today. If so, share with that person what God has done (or is still doing) in your heart.

Supplemental Reading:
❑ Colossians 3
❑ James 3:13-18

DAY 39
GOD'S VOICE IN SPIRITUAL GIFTS

Art Thomas

I don't think that everyone should focus all of their time on every gift, but I think that all of us are meant to at the very least experience all the gifts.

~ Blake Healy

1 Corinthians 12:7-11 — Now to each one the manifestation of the Spirit is given for the common good. To one there is given through the Spirit a message of wisdom, to another a message of knowledge by means of the same Spirit, to another faith by the same Spirit, to another gifts of healing by that one Spirit, to another miraculous powers, to another prophecy, to another distinguishing between spirits, to another speaking in different kinds of tongues, and to still another the interpretation of tongues. All these are the work of one and the same

Spirit, and He distributes them to each
one, just as He determines. (NIV)

THE LIST YOU JUST READ IS NOT CLOSED. MANY
other spiritual gifts are listed elsewhere in the Bible.
Today's lesson isn't so much a teaching about
spiritual gifts, though, as it is a teaching about how
God speaks through spiritual gifts.

In the beginning of the passage, we learn that
these actions of the Holy Spirit are "for the common
good." If we think gifts are only for the benefit of the
person being directly affected (like the person being
healed or the person being prophesied over), then we
are missing out on the good that is available to the
rest of us. Everyone is supposed to benefit from the
operation of God's Spirit among us. Whenever we
see the grace and power of God in action, He speaks
to us through it—sometimes directly and sometimes
indirectly.

God's direct speech to us comes through gifts
like prophecy or a "message of knowledge" (perhaps
better known as a "word of knowledge"). In the cases
of these gifts, a message or some information is
directly communicated from God. Both the person
operating in the gift and the person or people
receiving ministry experience the voice of God.

But all spiritual gifts reveal the indirect voice
of God. He is always revealing something about
Himself whenever He does anything in the earth.
When He heals, we learn about His compassion.
When He works a miracle, we learn about His
provision or protection. Even when a prophecy is
spoken directly to someone else, we who witness it
can still learn about God's love and nature. The gifts
of the Spirit speak.

Later in First Corinthians 12, Paul teaches that when we operate in spiritual gifts, we are being the "body" of Christ. Everything we do in partnership with the Holy Spirit reveals Jesus. When Jesus explained how the Holy Spirit operates, He said, "He will glorify Me because it is from Me that He will receive what He will make known to you." (See John 16:14.) The things the Holy Spirit gives are glimpses at Jesus.

Whether you're operating in a spiritual gift or watching the Holy Spirit in action through someone else, you are witnessing a revelation of Jesus. The Word is being made known by the Holy Spirit. God is speaking something, and there is therefore something to be learned.

For example, when we see a gift of faith in operation, we learn that God can be trusted beyond what we may have originally thought possible. When we see gifts of healing in operation, we learn about the power and will of God. When we see miracles happen, we discover that God is a faithful Provider or that He is more powerful than our problems. Every spiritual gift is a revelation of Jesus and should receive attention as an expression of the voice of God.

Hebrews 2:3-4 tells us that God "testifies" to the reality of the Gospel through spiritual gifts. Gifts point to the truth of grace. In fact, the root word for "gifts" in the original Greek language is the word for "grace." Gifts are expressions of our benevolent Father who loves to give good gifts to His children. (See Matthew 7:11 and James 1:17.)

Always be open to the Holy Spirit empowering you for whatever service is needed at a given time. Similarly, rejoice whenever He empowers someone else with a spiritual gift. And whenever He does—whether the recipient of the gift is you or someone else—take the time to think about what you experienced and search for the voice of God in whatever took place. God is speaking.

Prayer Starter:

- ❑ Thank God for being active among us today and for giving us His Holy Spirit.
- ❑ Ask the Holy Spirit to build your faith for spiritual gifts to happen through your life whenever He determines one would be useful.
- ❑ Ask God to work spiritual gifts through you and your church more frequently than He does now.

Journal Experience:

Turn back to page 40. In the second question on that page, you asked, "Jesus, what do You think of me?" Read what you wrote down. Does this line up with what you know of Scripture? Does it sound and feel like Jesus? If so, consider what this revelation teaches you about Jesus. What aspects of His nature are being made known? What is Jesus revealing about Himself in what He spoke about you?

_____

_____

_____

_____

_____

_____

_____

_____

_____

_____

_____

_____

_____

_____

_____

_____

_____

_____

Action Step:

Spiritual gifts are only healthy in an atmosphere of love. Our consistency in loving people makes us safe people to whom the Spirit can gladly distribute gifts. So practice love today. Ask God if there is someone specific in your life who He wants you to purposefully and lovingly serve today in a self-sacrificial way. If He doesn't direct you to anyone in particular, simply pick someone. "Love never fails."

Supplemental Reading:
❑   Romans 12:3-11
❑   1 Peter 4:7-11

DAY 40
GOD'S VOICE IN LEADERSHIP

Art Thomas

And so don't camp on the prophetic words that you've been given. Don't make those your hope. Make it your business — make it your pursuit — to conform to the image of the Son. That's what we're about. That's what we're for. Let me conform to the image of Jesus. Let me become as He is. Nothing else really matters. Nothing else matters. If I conform to His image, I'll be doing what I'm called to do.
~ R. Loren Sandford

> **Romans 12:6,8** — We have different gifts, according to the grace given to each of us. If your gift is....to lead, do it diligently...
> (NIV)

JESUS DOESN'T LEAD LIKE THE WORLD LEADS. IN THE same way, those of us in the Church who He has graced to lead do not lead like the world. If our leadership is an expression of Jesus, then our leadership speaks. Healthy leadership reveals Jesus.

Jesus made this point in Matthew 20:25-28: "You know that the rulers of the Gentiles lord it over them, and their high officials exercise authority over them. Not so with you. Instead, whoever wants to become great among you must be your servant, and whoever wants to be first must be your slave—just as the Son of Man did not come to be served, but to serve, and to give His life as a ransom for many." Christ-like leadership is service-based, not hierarchy-based.

There are plenty of leadership books that will teach you how to exercise authority over people, but that's how sinners lead sinners, not how Jesus leads. Worldly leadership is about imposing authority. Godly leadership is about being the first person into new territory so that others can benefit. Worldly leadership is a financier, sending an explorer into dangerous, uncharted lands. Godly leadership is taking the risk to blaze trails and let others reap the reward. Worldly leadership is a picture of a king hiding in a cave while his armies go to war. Godly leadership is a picture of a king on the frontlines of battle, leading the charge. Worldly leadership lets others pay the price while the leader reaps the rewards. Godly leadership takes up a cross, dies in the place of sinners, and gives us blessing after blessing that we don't deserve.

Godly leadership picks up its own cross first and only then invites others to "take up your cross and follow Me" (Matthew 16:24; Mark 8:34; Luke 9:23). That's how Jesus leads. He was the first to self-sacrifice. "While we were still sinners, Christ died for us" (Romans 5:8).

In practical terms, I lead in my home by

trying to be the first person to do the right thing. If there is frustration or unrest in my home, I try to be the first person to lay down my pride, seek Jesus, and find peace in Him. I then step back into the situation with a recalibrated heart, and His peace spreads to my wife and kids. Sometimes this means bowing out of an argument even when I know I'm right, but nothing exposes the truth in hindsight more than the light of Jesus infiltrating the situation. I've found more victory through self-surrender and love than I have ever found through clever arguments or harsh logic. (And lest anyone think too highly of me, I must admit that my wife is sometimes the first to do the right thing—and sometimes it's even one of my children!)

Leaders in the Church should be the first to repent, the first to forgive, the first to love, the first to serve, and so forth. These actions speak. They are prophetic pictures of Jesus that teach the rest of us about Him. After washing His disciples' feet, Jesus said, "You call me 'Teacher' and 'Lord,' and rightly so, for that is what I am. Now that I, your Lord and Teacher, have washed your feet, you also should wash one another's feet. I have set you an example that you should do as I have done for you" (John 13:13-15). Jesus was rightly called "Teacher" and "Lord," but He redefined those terms for all who would come after Him. Real leaders serve.

Leaders in the workforce should do the same. The best-run businesses are the ones where people feel valued and safe. Godly managers and business owners devote themselves to bettering the lives of their employees and helping them to grow and succeed, even when it will cost them personally. "The Good Shepherd lays down His life for the sheep" (John 10:11).

I own the publishing company that produced the book you have in your hands right now. I arguably did more work on this book than either of my co-authors (writing, editing, formatting, designing, etc.), but we share the royalties evenly with each other. We also give a portion of the profit to charity to be used for global missions work — caring for orphans, training pastors, and planting churches. I'm not saying everyone must run their businesses exactly like I do, but I do want you to know that I'm not just talking theories here. I practice what I'm preaching and hope it inspires business owners who read this book to think creatively about how to make their businesses more of a blessing to others than they already are.

Not only can godly leadership itself be prophetic, but sometimes we who lead need God's direction and wisdom. If we ask God for wisdom, He will give it (James 1:5). Sometimes that wisdom will come to us directly, but He may also speak through someone else in our life. Keep your ears open for godly wisdom in any form. Moses, for example, was in a leadership crisis until his father-in-law, Jethro, gave him wise counsel for how to lead the people well (Exodus 18:13-27).

Every believer is a leader in some regard. If you're not leading a church, you might lead a small group. You might lead your family. You might lead a business or a work group. But all of us — regardless of status or social influence — are called to lead the lost to Jesus.

The only way to lead well is to let Jesus lead you well. As we surrender to Him, He lives His life through us and leads by the power of the Holy Spirit.

Prayer Starter:

- ❑ Praise God for His Kingship in your life. Tell Him what it means to you that "God" would serve His creation. Thank Him for His love.
- ❑ Ask Jesus to teach you to lead like He leads.
- ❑ Ask the Holy Spirit to show you any area of your life that is not honoring and valuing others above yourself. Ask the Lord for help in surrendering that area of life to His purposes.

Journal Experience:

Hebrews 13:7 says, "Remember your leaders, who spoke the word of God to you. Consider the outcome of their way of life and imitate their faith."

In obedience to this scripture, think of someone who has spiritually led you well in the past or present—perhaps a pastor, a mentor, a parent, or a caregiver who has revealed Jesus with their actions. Write down some observations about their way of life that likely enabled them to reveal Jesus as effectively as they did.

_____

_____

_____

_____

_____

_____

_____

_____

_____

_____

_____

_____

_____

_____

_____

_____

_____

_____

_____

Action Step:

Encourage someone who God has given leadership in your life. Whether they're perfectly representing Jesus or not is irrelevant. Identify the traits in their lives that do remind you of Jesus, and point those things out to them. Thank them for representing Jesus in that way to you.

Supplemental Reading:
- ❑ Philippians 2:5-8
- ❑ 1 Timothy 3:1-7
- ❑ 1 Peter 5:2-5

What Now?

Congratulations on completing this entire 40-Day journey! We have no doubt that you have been impacted on some level by the teachings and challenges from each day of the study.

There are three things we would like to recommend for you to do next:

1. Watch the movie *Voice of God* a second time. Many people are so overwhelmed during their first viewing that they miss much of the message. Watching it again—after having completed this study—is sure to be a different experience and may bring out new insights that you had not previously noticed.
2. Consider hosting a 10-week small group study about hearing God, with direction from the DVD curriculum available at SupernaturalTruth.com.

You can even use this book as supplemental reading that corresponds to each week's lesson.
3. Keep spreading the message of Jesus Christ's love toward everyone and His power to save, heal, and set free!

It has been an honor to have been welcomed to speak into your life for the past few weeks, and we pray that God guards the seeds that have been planted through this study so that you bear much fruit in His Kingdom. Be blessed as you minister the full Gospel of Jesus Christ wherever He sends you!

Art Thomas
James Loruss
Jonathan Ammon

About the Authors

Art Thomas

Art Thomas is a missionary-evangelist who has preached the Gospel in many diverse settings spanning from the inner city of Brooklyn, New York, to the bush of Africa. Now serving as the president and CEO of *Wildfire Ministries International*, Art has seen thousands of salvations and miraculous healings since stepping into itinerant ministry in April of 2011. He is the director and producer of the movies *Paid in Full* and *Voice of God* and has been actively involved in training thousands of believers to minister in the power of the Holy Spirit since 2009.

Art is the author of several books, including *The Word of Knowledge in Action: A Practical Guide for the Supernatural Church*. He lives with his wife, Robin, and their two boys, Josiah and Jeremiah, in Canton, Michigan.

James Loruss

James Loruss is the vice president and Chief Operating Officer of *Wildfire Ministries International* and is the co-Director of the movies *Paid in Full* and *Voice of God.* James studied film music scoring at Madonna University, which provided the initial inspiration for the first film that he and Art would go on to make.

James has preached to hundreds in America and thousands in Africa and has been actively involved in ministering healing and prophetic words since 2009. His greatest passions — besides the salvation of the lost — include the Church understanding identity in Christ and the love of the Father. James lives with his wife, Connie, in Novi, Michigan.

Jonathan Ammon

Jonathan Ammon is a ministry associate with *Wildfire Ministries International* who has traveled extensively (in America and Uganda) with Art Thomas and James Loruss and also helped with the filming of the movies *Paid in Full* and *Voice of God.* He has devoted the past several years of his life to a 2-square-mile city within downtown Detroit, Michigan, called Hamtramck. Within those 2 square miles are 14 mosques with roughly 40% of the population having been born overseas. It is currently known as the only city in the United States where the Muslim "call to prayer" is openly broadcast five times a day.

Jonathan, along with his wife, Tatiana,

teaches English as a Second Language to immigrants (mostly from Yemen and Bangladesh) using the Bible as a study tool. He conducts street evangelism, starts Bible studies in homes, and is actively involved in prophetic and healing ministries while training other believers to do the same things in Jesus' name. Most of his efforts are devoted to establishing a movement of evangelistic, self-replicating gatherings of Christians throughout the region that will spread the Gospel faster than the current birth rate.

For more information about
Wildfire Ministries International,
please visit
www.WildfireMin.org

For more information about
Supernatural Truth Productions,
please visit
www.SupernaturalTruth.com

APPENDIX A:

Overview of Some of the Ways God Speaks

Art Thomas

FIRST OF ALL, IF YOU'RE A CHRISTIAN, THEN YOU have already heard God's voice:

> John 6:44-45—No one can come to Me unless the Father who sent Me draws him; and I will raise him up on the last day. It is written in the prophets, 'And they shall all be taught of God.' Everyone who has heard and learned from the Father comes to Me." (NASB)

Hearing God's voice is amazingly simple! He is regularly speaking—it's just up to us to pay attention. The following list of "ways God speaks" is not exhaustive—you may discover more ways as you go through life. What matters is that we are constantly looking for His voice in all situations.

Here are some of the ways God speaks to us:

Externally

NOTE: The "external" ways God speaks to us come from the outside. They're less intimate than the "personal" ways listed on the next page, but they are just as important. We need to listen for God to speak in any way He chooses.

1. **Creation** (Romans 1:20)
2. **Circumstances** (Hebrews 12:7-11)
3. **Signs and wonders** (Hebrews 2:4)
4. **Angels** (Angelic encounters were very common throughout the whole Bible.)
5. **Through others**
   a. *Word of Knowledge*
   b. *Word of Wisdom*
   c. *Prophecy*
   d. *Tongues and Interpretation*
   e. *Preaching & Teaching*
   f. *Music*
6. **The Church** (Ephesians 3:10-11)
7. **The Bible** (2 Peter 1:20,21)

Internally / Personally

1. **Still, small voice** (1 Kings 19:12)
2. **Impressions, sensing, or perception** (Acts 27:10)
3. **Physical sensations** (Luke 8:46)
4. **Spiritual gifts** (1 Corinthians 12-14)
    a. *Spontaneous Prophetic Word*
    b. *Word of Knowledge*
    c. *Word of Wisdom*
    d. *Tongues and Interpretation*
5. **Visions**
    a. *"Closed Visions" – a picture in the mind (whether symbolic or literal)*
    b. *"Open Visions" – perceived as being part of your natural surroundings*
6. **Dreams** (Job 33:14-16)
7. **Audible voice** (John 12:29)
8. **Trances** (Acts 10:9-17)
9. **Divine encounters** (Numbers 12:7-8)

For more detail about many of these topics, see Section 2 of this book: "Some of the Ways God Speaks."

APPENDIX B:

Staying Real and Grounded

Art Thomas

THERE'S AN OLD PHRASE I REMEMBER HEARING multiple times as I was learning to operate in prophetic ministry: "Be careful you don't become so heavenly minded that you're of no earthly good."

My gut reaction was to say, "It's better than being so earthly minded that I'm no heavenly good!"

But that's not really what the people were talking about. What they really meant is what I have now witnessed to be true. The problem isn't with being heavenly-minded. As a matter of fact, we are commanded to set our minds on things above. (See Colossians 3:1-2.) The problem is that many believers—in their pursuit of prophetic encounters—have slipped away from reality and into the realm of mere fantasy.

Despite our best intentions, if we're not

careful, we can create a false concept of the world in which everything we imagine is assumed to be true. The results can range anywhere from confusion to ineffectiveness to outright destruction of our lives and ministries.

What follows in the coming sections are bits of wisdom derived from personal experience. I offer them here as warning signs that will keep you on the path of genuine encounters with God and true prophetic ministry. I'm sure this list is not complete, but I do believe it's a good start. Please consider each point and allow the Holy Spirit to help you guard against deception.

Discern the Prophetic Voices around You

I really hate to say this, but the fact is that the prophetic movement often attracts people with mental illness. I want to be careful with that statement because history has proven that many genuinely prophetic people have been wrongfully considered mentally ill. But perhaps that's why such things happen — we find it hard to distinguish between those who are having genuine encounters with God and those whose minds are either not well or, in some cases, tormented or influenced by demons.

Just because someone claims to have heard from God does not mean that they have. It's vitally important that we watch the fruit of people's lives. What comes of their "revelations"? Do they produce spiritual health and even positive results in the physical realm? Or do they tend to bring more confusion or frustration to those influenced by the person?

I once met an older man who — although a little socially awkward — seemed like a normal believer who loved Jesus. I had a great conversation with him about Scripture. Everything about this guy seemed like he was an average Christian who might attend any average church.

But as our conversation was winding down, he said, "I want to show you something." The man opened one side of his coat as though he were a shady street vender selling stolen watches. "These are my spiritual weapons that the Lord gave me. Can you see them?"

I saw absolutely nothing and didn't want to lie to the guy, but I also wasn't ready to write him off as nutty just yet. Everything had seemed cool so far. "Sorry, I don't."

"They're spiritual throwing daggers. I just walk down the street, and whenever I see a demon, I reach in my coat and throw them at the demons. I also have love potions that I can throw at people so they can feel God's love."

Suddenly and swiftly, he pretended to yank something from inside his coat and throw it at me with a big smile on his face. "Did you feel that?" he asked with wide eyes.

"Not really," I answered.

"Well, then," he replied, "it seems you're not as discerning as I thought you were. I can't meet with you anymore."

I was so confused and so deeply bothered. It seemed that the only people this guy would allow in his life were the ones who would affirm him in his delusions. God doesn't reveal His love through invisible love potions; He reveals His love through people actually serving others in Jesus' name. He doesn't defeat the enemy through invisible daggers; He defeats the enemy through the blood of Jesus, the word of our testimony, and acts of faith-filled obedience (Revelation 12:11).

It's healthy to allow people into your life who will question your encounters with God. Even if what you experience is true, you will learn to let the fruit prove you right rather than merely wanting validation from people.

If you're surrounding yourself with people who believe everything you say, then you risk slipping into deception. But if you surround yourself with people who desire the Truth and sometimes question your experiences, you'll learn to discern better, you'll learn to articulate your experiences better, you'll learn to love people better, and you'll learn to value genuine fruit that proves the reality of true spiritual encounters.

Healing from Inner Wounds

I once met a minister who was interested in partnering with me for making a larger impact on the world around me. At the time I was a worship leader and youth leader at a small, rural church. I knew I was called to bigger things, and this guy seemed like he might be providing the perfect path to that end. He already had an established ministry, he believed everything I said to him about encounters I'd had with the Lord, and he was even well-respected throughout my home state (at least among many in Charismatic churches).

As I was praying about how to partner with

the man in ministry, the Lord gave me a vision of a Purple Heart medal—the award given to members of the United States military who have been wounded in battle. The Lord spoke to me and said, "This man has been wounded in battle and hasn't healed. If you fight alongside him, you will be wounded too."

As I dialogued further with the Lord, He showed me that many people in Pentecostal and Charismatic churches—which includes many people in today's "prophetic movement"—have experienced a lot of pain because close friends, family, and even pastors have refused to believe their experiences. Many have been rejected by those closest to them. As a result, many have recoiled from engaging with those who wounded them and, in pain, banded together with people who had similar experiences.

When I thought about it, all the people around this particular leader showed signs of having been wounded as well. In fact, the guy with the "spiritual daggers" that I mentioned in the previous section was one of his followers.

When we've experienced the wound of rejection from other believers, it's only natural to desire never to do the same thing to anyone else. But the way this often plays out is that we blindly believe everything those people say (so as not to reject them) and ultimately wind up doing a disservice to them, ourselves, and everyone around us.

We need to allow the Lord to heal any wounds in our hearts from rejection—especially as it pertains to encounters we believe we've had with the Lord. Only then can we actually help others who have been wounded.

I'm not saying that we need to go around telling people that they're wrong or delusional, nor do I believe we need to heartlessly toss out statements like, "You're just wounded." If the person actually is wounded in such a way, then they'll probably take your words as yet another rejection and back away (just like my friend with the daggers did when I simply "didn't feel" something). That's not the solution.

A better solution is to be able to say something like, "I love you and consider you a brother in the kingdom. I'm not yet convinced of what you're saying, but because of love, I'm willing to look into it and take time to discern."

About a year into our little, rural church plant, around twenty of us were meeting in a local family's basement. The husband in the family said, "I feel like we're supposed to do a 'Jericho march' around the pool outside, and then God's going to give us all breakthrough." If you're not familiar with the term, the man was saying that we were supposed to march seven times around their above-ground pool, just as Joshua and the Israelites marched around the walls of Jericho, causing the walls to collapse and the city to be overthrown.

My pastor responded by saying, "I'll be honest with you. I'm not sensing that or feeling that at all, but I'm willing to do it out of love for you."

All twenty of us went outside and marched around that pool seven times. Thankfully, the walls of the pool didn't collapse. But neither did it bring the miraculous breakthrough that was promised. One of the new believers later told us that she felt like an absolute fool and considered never coming back except that our pastor had voiced that we were doing it in love for the man who wanted us to go out there. The "prophetic word" bore no fruit—in fact, it would have borne bad fruit if not for my pastor's wise words of love.

I wish I could say that this one instance was enough to heal the man's heart and help him see that he wasn't hearing God clearly, but he and his wife ended up leaving our church a few months later due to unrelated offenses.

If you've experienced wounds and rejection from others — especially in regard to prophetic experiences and encounters with God — it is vital that you process through those experiences with the Lord and let Him bring healing. Ask God to tell you what He thinks about what happened to you. Ask Him how the people should have responded if they had been listening to Him. Ask Him about His loving desires for the people who wronged you. Choose to forgive them in your heart and release them from any anger, hatred, disgust, or other negative emotions. Repent of your own bitterness, receive the forgiveness of the Lord for yourself, and take a moment to pray for those people and speak blessing over their lives in Jesus' name.

Value Fruit over Experiences

After all that I've written so far, this seems like it should go without saying. Yet I cannot emphasize it enough. If the value is in the experience and not the fruit that comes out of it, then you run the risk of busying yourself with fruitless experiences that may not even be real.

I do want to bring some clarity here, though. A deeper love for God is good fruit. A discovery of His love for you is good fruit. So just because an encounter with the Lord may not have produced any results in the physical realm doesn't mean that it doesn't have fruit. All I'm saying is that if we're having lots of "spiritual encounters" but are not actually growing in our walks with the Lord, then we need to question those encounters. Throughout Scripture, we see a pattern that encounters with God always produce good fruit—unless the person rebels against whatever God has directed.

I should also note that I'm not instructing you to give little value to experiences. On the contrary, we should highly value every spiritual encounter we have with the Lord. However, I am still saying that no matter how highly we may value our spiritual experiences, we need to value lasting fruit above those experiences.

I've had several unbelievable encounters with God, including a handful of heavenly experiences (only a couple of which do I feel I have permission to share with others). But the thing that causes me to value those encounters most is the fruit that they produced in my life. God was directly teaching me about true grace and identity in Christ long before these became popular topics in the Church, and it deeply affected the way I lived and taught others. Some of these encounters brought deep healing to my life. Others encouraged me in such a way that they propelled me forward in ministry to others.

Only on a couple occasions can I remember a spiritual encounter that bore no fruit for me and left no physical evidence. And to this day, no matter how real those experiences felt in the moment, I'm still not sure if they were actually God. I haven't completely written them off, but I do question them and refuse to teach from them or let them shape my theology.

Jesus said that we would be able to identify false prophets by their fruit. I would argue that we can also identify our own encounters as true or false based on the fruit that is either produced or not when we act on those revelations.

Call Things What They Are

If the feeling you have is vague, let people know that it's vague. If the feeling you have is specific, let people know it's specific. If you have a feeling that what you're sensing might be nothing more than observation and not spiritual, say so.

Far too often I have seen people disregard this bit of wisdom. The result is that people stop taking the gift of prophecy seriously.

In his book *Purifying the Prophetic,* R. Loren Sandford writes about how human beings have an innate, God-given ability to "read" people. (Those who have seen the 2-part film associated with this book have seen him explain this in Episode 2.) Unfortunately, many of us use that natural human ability in the name of prophetic ministry and end up giving false words and false hope. People may be amazed that we were able to tell them details about their lives or even explain back to them their desires or their passions in ministry, but we've done nothing more than naturally read the person and reflect back their own hearts to them.

I try to be very careful about how I word things when I think I might just be reading a person. I'll say things like, "I get the sense that you're the type of person who..." Perhaps this is what the woman at the well was doing when she said to Jesus,

"Sir, I perceive that you are a prophet" (John 4:19).

Likewise, when the sense I have from the Lord is vague, I tell people so. Sometimes I'm certain that I've had a vision or dream from the Lord but uncertain about the interpretation. In these cases, I tell people exactly what I saw and what I "think" it may have meant.

Most importantly, after you've been practicing hearing God's voice for a long time and He has trained you to grow in your discernment, there's nothing wrong with speaking with certainty about what you've heard. I definitely reserve this for those who are a bit more seasoned, though, because I can't tell you how many times I've felt certain about whatever I was perceiving and then found out I was wrong. Some have suggested that it takes as long as 40 years to raise up an effective and "solid" prophetic minister. I don't know if I'm yet convinced of the exact number, but I would definitely agree that we need to exercise caution when it comes to the things we present as being "definitely" from God.

Guard Against Prideful Inconsistency

As I write these words, I just listened to an audio recording of a supposed prophetic word about the United States, along with an interview of the person who gave the word. Time will tell whether or not the word comes true, but something about the interview struck me.

The person was making the case that we shouldn't speak against God's plan. He identified a public figure in the media who had contradicted his message and that same night became sick. In this man's mind, this media figure had been punished by God for working against God's plan.

The irony, though, was that only a few minutes later, the man said that he had been sick for several years, and this was evidence that he had been doing the right thing (because apparently he was under some sort of spiritual attack from the enemy).

Not knowing this man, I can't judge his heart and say exactly what was happening, but I thought this was a pretty straightforward illustration of what I've seen many times among prophetic people. When it comes to ourselves and the people with whom we agree, sickness and calamity are considered spiritual attack; but when it comes to those with whom we disagree, sickness and calamity are considered God's punishment.

This sort of prideful inconsistency is a sad irony that undermines the prophetic movement and causes people to look at us with skepticism and disdain.

It's okay to admit that we don't always know why bad things happen. It's okay to admit that we may be under the Lord's discipline or that those we dislike might be under spiritual attack. It's also okay for sickness and calamity to have no spiritual cause whatsoever and be nothing more than the trials of living in a fallen world. Just because you can make a connection in your mind that makes sense to you doesn't mean that it's true. It's vital that we have maturity, humility, and discernment from the Lord. Don't let the enemy trick you into drawing assumptions with your carnal mind that validate you in your pride.

Take Responsibility for What You Say

If something you said prophetically didn't come to pass, don't try to switch things around to convince yourself or others that it did. In Episode 2 of our film *Voice of God,* R. Loren Sandford called these "rubber prophecies" that we "stretch to fit." I can't tell you how many times I've seen someone promise some sort of destruction coming to America only to blame the absence of it on the fact that people must have prayed to keep it away. This is cowardly and wrong.

If I make a predictive statement that I believe is from the Lord, then I hold myself accountable before the Lord if that word doesn't come to pass, and I will repent publicly for my error. But far too often, we see ministers selling books and DVDs that promise something big will happen at a certain time, stirring up all manner of fear and urgency in the Body of Christ; and yet those things never actually come to pass. No apology — just new books later.

Until the people who make such predictions take responsibility publicly for their errors, prophetic people will continue to be mocked by those who watch from the outside, and prophetic ministry will never be taken seriously by the masses. I've heard prophetic ministers complain that today's society doesn't take the word of the Lord seriously, but I would argue that neither do many of the ministers.

If you make a prediction in the name of Jesus that does not come to pass, then have the fortitude and the maturity to renounce your previous words to the same audience. Perhaps in time we can rebuild trust with people in the world, and they might just begin to take our words seriously again.

Value Relationships with Mature Believers

Much has been said already in this book about the value of human relationships. (See especially Day 14, Day 19, and Day 28.) I'm not interested in re-hashing all that information, so you can read it there.

I would, however, like to testify to the tremendous healing that has taken place in my own heart through deep connections with mature believers—people who loved me despite my rough edges and created a safe environment for me to be vulnerable, transparent, and authentic. These people loved me in such a way that I didn't feel a need to impress them or earn their favor. I never felt an urge to fabricate a prophetic encounter or to try to convince them to be as amazed with my revelations as I was.

This spiritual family also lovingly challenged me when my words didn't pass the scrutinizing tests Scripture tells us to follow for judging revelation. (See Section 4 of this book and also Day 28.) They knew the Bible well and weren't afraid to push back on things I taught. This trained me to also study Scripture and to be more discerning with my own experiences and ideas before delivering them.

I highly recommend that you find at least one person who will lovingly question you when the things you say don't sound right to their ears. You may even be right, but this will push you to search the Scriptures and make the biblical case for your revelation rather than being content with whatever idea came to your mind. God's words are worth wrestling with. They're worth challenging. If they're truly from God, they'll pass the test. And the rest will be thrown out, leading to greater prophetic purity.

Learn to Study the Scriptures Well

Many people's eyes gloss over when you start to talk about academic words like "exegesis" and "hermeneutics." But these words, which basically refer to proper interpretation methods for understanding Scripture, are worth studying.

There is a strange tendency among many Pentecostal and Charismatic Christians to deride academia. We like to jokingly replace the word "seminary" with "cemetery" because we have seen so many fired-up believers go to Bible college and come back spiritually dead. We praise those who have pastored for 50 years and never went to school.

Thankfully, many Bible schools now exist under the direction of Spirit-filled, loving, faithful believers who practice their theology and don't just talk about it. Biblical training is not a bad thing.

All that said, you don't need to go to Bible school to learn some basic interpretation techniques — things like considering the genre of the passage in question, considering the intended audience, and reading things in context of the larger message being presented.

This topic is larger than I can adequately teach in a couple paragraphs, so for those interested, I would recommend to you a book by Gordon D. Fee and Douglas Stuart titled *How to Read the Bible for All It's Worth*. This book covers academic topics of interpretation in a down-to-earth way that is approachable for most non-academics. Your spiritual growth and Biblical understanding will greatly benefit from reading it.

APPENDIX C:

The Difference Between Old and New Testament Prophecy

Art Thomas

MANY HAVE NOTED THAT PAUL'S GUIDELINES OF "strengthening, encouraging and comfort" (1 Corinthians 14:3) seem to not apply to most Old Testament prophecy. Some have pointed out the contrast with what God told the prophet Jeremiah. God said He had placed His words in Jeremiah's mouth and appointed him "over nations and kingdoms to uproot and tear down, to destroy and overthrow, to build and to plant" (Jeremiah 1:9-10). That sounds way more destructive and formative than "strengthening, encouraging, and comfort!" Indeed, this seems to be more in line with what we see throughout the Old Testament examples of prophecy.

Technically, nothing truly changed. The role of prophetic ministry has always been so speak what God is saying. And what God says—from the Old Testament until today—has always provided strengthening, encouragement, and comfort to those whose trust is in Him.

In the Old Testament, prophecy was speaking what God was saying for the audience to whom He said to speak it. And in the New Testament, prophecy is still speaking what God is saying for the audience to whom He says to speak it. Prophecy itself hasn't actually changed.

But that doesn't explain what we do see as differences between Old and New Testament prophecy. These things, I would suggest, are most likely found in understanding the intended audience and recognizing what God is regularly speaking differently today than He did then.

Knowing Your Audience

Biblically, God sometimes chooses to speak certain things through one person while choosing not to speak them through another. God's word to Jeremiah was not a definition of "prophecy" but a definition of Jeremiah's specific calling, describing the level of things he would be prophesying and to whom. God appointed Jeremiah for a specific purpose that is not necessarily all of our purposes.

Gifts of the Spirit are distributed to each one as the Spirit determines (1 Corinthians 12:4, 11). As we have seen throughout this book, every believer has the ability to hear God, and therefore every believer can hear God for someone else and prophesy. But not every believer is called to the same audience. Not every believer has been granted the same platform or sphere of earthly influence. And therefore what God wants to say through each believer will likely vary as well.

For example, unless God intends to give me a meeting with the President of the United States, He probably is not going to give me a prophetic word for the President. I don't have any influence there. But I do have a wide readership on my web site and Facebook, and occasionally (though admittedly rarely), God will speak something to me of wide-scale relevance for the Body of Christ at large. Some of these prophetic words have been shared on social media by thousands of people, and I don't take that responsibility lightly. I know who my audience is, and so does God. I speak to the ones He has given me, and I trust Him to bring the right readers. My goal is to be faithful to honor the influence He has given me so that He can regularly speak through me on that scale.

But for many years, my influence was nothing larger than my local church. What God spoke through me during that season was always either to them or to individuals I knew. I didn't try to build my audience or reach beyond what God had given me, and I only ever spoke to a larger crowd as the Lord directed. Still to this day, God most frequently speaks through me to my local church and to individuals around me.

I don't believe I'm a prophet in the biblical sense because I know I'm most called to train and equip the Body of Christ in different things (Ephesians 4:11-13); but I am a Christian, and

Christians are prophetic. God will speak through every Christian in whatever arena He has given that Christian influence. Prophecy, dreams, and visions are for every believer, regardless of age or gender (Joel 2:28). Not every Christian is a prophet because not every Christian is called to train and equip other believers in that way. But every Christian is prophetic, and every Christian has a unique sphere of influence that God desperately wants to reach.

Jeremiah was appointed "over nations and kingdoms" (Jeremiah 1:10). Isaiah was sent to the people of Israel (Isaiah 6:9). Jonah was sent to Nineveh (Jonah 1:2). The reason Old Testament prophecy seems so different from New Testament prophecy is that our biggest examples are people through whom God wanted to speak some specific things to some rather large audiences. We forget that the Old Testament also contains some less dramatic, more personal words of prophecy that are probably more relatable to most of us today.

What is your audience? In a broad sense, you have been sent to the entire world (Matthew 28:19; Mark 16:15; Acts 1:8), but that commission is for all of us collectively. Jesus didn't intend for each individual believer to preach in every country on the planet. But in a specific sense, what is your current sphere of influence? Prophesy there as He leads. To what extent does God want to extend your influence? The only way to truly find out is to remain faithful with the influence He has given you now, and wait for Him to lead anywhere else. If He intends to speak through you to a different audience, He will accomplish it — usually by giving you simple steps of obedience to follow until it happens.

God has New Things to Say

One major difference that does exist between most examples of Old Testament prophecy and New Testament prophecy is what God is saying. For example, God is no longer foretelling the coming of a Jewish Messiah. Jesus has already come. This fact that Jesus has come has significant implications on prophetic ministry today.

For one thing, there's a new audience in the earth called "the Church." Prior to Jesus coming, those who were righteous "by grace through faith" seemed to be anomalies. Most people tried and failed to follow an external Law. Not until the New Testament was that Law written on our hearts so that we could actually be transformed and know the Lord (Jeremiah 31:31-34). It stands to reason, therefore, that the things God is going to speak to the Church will be more in line with the things God spoke to righteous, faith-filled people in the Old Testament— things like His promises to Abraham, His assurances to David, or His wisdom to Solomon.

Today's faith-filled people—the Church— gather into smaller family units that we call "churches." A look at the first three chapters of Revelation should indicate to us that what God has to say to each of these family units will vary from one church to the next. One local spiritual family differs from the next, and so God has different things to say to each of us. Revelation 1-3 also shows us that God still speaks corrective words, but He speaks to His people with encouragement as well—always pointing out what they're doing right.

Another new thing God speaks today is in reference to how He interacts with the wicked. In the

Old Testament, death and destruction for sin were a common refrain. The words God spoke through the prophets of old often brought harsh judgment on sinners—even destroying whole nations.

But in the New Testament, the only judgment we see is a future act that will come upon the whole world, not a constant refrain pointed at nations or people groups. When Jesus read from the scroll of the prophet Isaiah and said that the prophecy was fulfilled that day in Him, He stopped reading mid-sentence. He said that He came to declare "the year of the Lord's favor," but He omitted "and the day of the vengeance of our God." (Compare Luke 4:16-21 to Isaiah 61:1-2.) Indeed, Jesus came giving abundant life (John 10:10) and spent very little time talking about the day of wrath that would one day come.

During this New Testament time, God is holding back His future wrath for as long as possible so that as many as possible can be saved (2 Peter 3:3-13). His kindness, tolerance, and patience are leading people to repentance (Romans 2:4).

The Gospel—specifically the cross of Christ—makes known God's wrath against all the sin of humanity (Romans 1:16-18), but God's wrath against sinners is being withheld at the moment until a future date that only the Father knows.

Read the following scripture carefully, and note what Peter says about the words God spoke in the past compared to the words He speaks today:

> **2 Peter 3:3-7 –** Above all, you must understand that in the last days scoffers will come, scoffing and following their own evil desires. They will say, "Where is this 'coming' He

promised? Ever since our ancestors died, everything goes on as it has since the beginning of creation." But they deliberately forget that long ago *by God's word* the heavens came into being and the earth was formed out of water and by water. By these waters also the world of that time was deluged and destroyed. *By the same word* the present heavens and earth are *reserved* for fire, *being kept* for the day of judgment and destruction of the ungodly. (NIV, emphasis added)

Do you see it? The "word" God is speaking today is a word of preservation—withholding judgment for as long as possible while the Church carries out the Great Commission. Along these same lines, Hebrews 1:3 tells us that Jesus—the perfect revelation of the Father—is "sustaining all things by His powerful word." God is sustaining the earth—keeping it from judgment until a future day of wrath.

Many Christians throughout the centuries have prophesied impending national judgments that never came. If they had simply realized what the Bible said about the things God is presently speaking, they would have had better discernment. Whenever people claim that earthquakes, hurricanes, tsunamis, tornadoes, wildfires, and other natural disasters are God's judgment, it's usually because they don't understand what God is now speaking in the earth. Perhaps an over-fascination with the Old Testament or spiritual immaturity has kept them blind to the mercy, patience, and preservation of God in the New Testament.

The one time James and John wanted to call down fire and destroy a village of sinners who had rejected the Gospel, Jesus rebuked them, saying, "You do not know what manner of spirit you are of. For the Son of Man did not come to destroy men's lives but to save them" (Luke 9:51-56, NKJV). Any person who prophesies or "ministers" death and destruction is partnering with the wrong spirit. God's speech is currently in the work of sustaining and preserving.

The Gospel, Revealed

Finally, it is important to note that the Gospel has now been revealed. In the Old Testament, the mystery of the Gospel was concealed (Romans 16:25-27). Even Jesus spoke in confusing parables prior to His death and resurrection (Matthew 13:10-17). But now our role is to fearlessly make it known (Ephesians 6:19).

In the Old Testament, God spoke in veiled terms about the Messiah who would come. Then Jesus came as the perfect revelation of the Father (Hebrews 1:1-3). Jesus is still today revealing the Father with full clarity, but now He does it through an obedient, faith-filled Church. As we choose union with Jesus in His death (considering our old, sinful lives to be dead), we can experience union with Jesus in His life (1 Corinthians 6:17; Galatians 2:20; Ephesians 2:6). Our faithful proclamation of the Gospel is a greater revelation than the entire Old Testament because it clearly reveals Christ.

I pray we all take seriously our prophetic, New-Testament role in the earth.

Supernatural Evangelism Pitfalls

Jeremiah Johnson
Used with Permission

FOR MANY YEARS, I WAS PERSONALLY INVOLVED with numerous prophetic/supernatural schools and churches from around the USA who would weekly go out to do prophetic and supernatural evangelism in different cities and regions.

I can honestly say that the first 10 years were incredible and nothing less than exhilarating. Watching people encounter the love of God for the very first time is amazing. We saw too many physical healings, demons being cast out, and powerful words of knowledge go forth to count. From setting up "Free Spiritual Reading" tents to simply handing out bottles of water and asking people if we could pray with them to try to lure them in for a supernatural encounter with God, I have both experienced and led many teams and seen a lot!

However, at about the ten-year mark of walking in this realm on a consistent basis, I believe God began to open up my eyes to some great deceptions concerning what I was doing, and I still consistently see and hear what I am about to share across the country today. IT DEEPLY BREAKS MY HEART! My hope in sharing what was revealed to me is to help those going out to do supernatural evangelism—and even those teaching it—to make some course adjustments and seek the Lord personally on these matters.

Here are 4 areas of deception that were revealed to me by the Holy Spirit concerning what I was doing and teaching in the supernatural/ prophetic evangelism realm:

1. The Gifts of the Holy Spirit

As I took a hard look at the role of the gifts of the Holy Spirit in the New Testament, I was shocked at what I found. The gifts of the Holy Spirit were only used for two purposes: (1) in a community and relational context among saints to promote unity and help them draw near the presence of God and (2) in an evangelistic setting to draw people INTO that community.

In other words, to demonstrate the gifts of the Holy Spirit on the streets without desiring to bring people into community and relationship with the body of Christ is unbiblical and deceptive. And to take it a step further, it seemed about seventy-five percent of the people with whom I did supernatural evangelism for many years did not attend a local church faithfully themselves and knew nothing of Christian community living.

Therefore, it is a violation to demonstrate the supernatural to the world without clearly trying to draw them into a community setting where relationship and unity can be formed. If you are going out trying to win souls, prophesy to people, and lay hands on them for healing without strongly encouraging and providing them with the correct avenues to get plugged into a community of believers where strong discipleship is taking place, I ask you to repent and turn from this deception.

2. Healing and Prophetic Showmanship

I cannot count on how many occasions I have seen people healed and prophetic words given without a presentation of the Gospel that includes asking people to repent of their sins. I have personally (which I have now repented of) and also taken teams all over the USA where we laid hands on the sick and crippled, saw them healed as we talked to them about the love of God and the work of the Cross, but yet never told them that they had to repent of their sins and live a consecrated life unto the Lord.

It's almost like we developed a culture where people were addicted to prophesying, healing the sick, and "demonstrating the love of God" but got more of a kick out of watching people encounter God than actually leading them to Christ. (I hope that makes sense).

Over the years, among many of us who were "gifted," it became like a game. Who could prophesy the most accurate, in-depth word or who could get the best healing?

Please, if you are reading this, take this seriously. I will not name the supernatural schools or leaders, but this type of thinking is so rampant, it would make you sick. Healings, prophecies, and the love of God — without a mention of holiness, righteous living, or the need to repent of sins — will produce people who seek an outward touch but reject inward transformation. They want goose bumps and stimulation but run from trials and testing.

If you are praying for healing and prophesying to people but not preaching the gospel and telling them that they must die to their flesh and pick up their cross and follow Jesus, I ask you to repent and turn from this deception.

3. Worshipping Miracles vs. Worshipping the God of Miracles

Another area of deception that God showed me I was walking in was my obsession with the miraculous outside of a true obsession for Jesus Christ. I found myself more eager to pray and release miracles than I was to pray to the God of miracles. I began to point people more to miracle-power than the God of miracle-power. Even in my language and speech, I had little to no revelation of the person of God, yet I had no problem "demonstrating" His works.

It all culminated for me when I went to sleep

one night and had a dream about hell. There the Holy Spirit showed me not only miracle-workers who went to hell because they never knew the Lord, but He showed me thousands of people who had received His miracle-working power when they lived yet had never truly given their heart and life to Him.

If you are addicted to miracles and the prophetic but do not possess a true obsession with Jesus Christ, I ask you to repent and turn from this deception.

4. Prophetic Activation and Impartation

Probably the strongest area of deception that I walked in was the zeal to activate and impart to people the prophetic anointing without spending any time teaching them about the character and nature of God or the need for their own character transformation. I was (or they were) so eager to lay hands (or have hands laid on them) and show them how to "do the stuff" that holding their feet to the fire regarding their own sin and lack of revelation of who God is was never addressed.

I realized over the years that I was actually causing collateral damage rather than releasing assets to the world. Many of these people "walked in the supernatural" for a season but ended up embracing loose living and no longer even serve the Lord. They were totally unprepared for real life situations where trial and testing simply do not go away with one prayer.

If you are training and activating students into the prophetic and supernatural without preaching holiness and living righteously before the

Lord (by grace through faith), I ask you to repent and turn from this deception.

Know Jesus

I have repented and will continue to repent of those years of walking in the deception that plagues so much of the "supernatural evangelism" that we have witnessed in recent years. If but one person wakes up to the reality that I am talking about and sees their own deception or helps another see theirs, it will be well worth it to me!

I will close with the words of my friend Loren Sandford and pray that those who have read this will either be on guard or—if you are doing what I mentioned above—repent of the deception that you are walking in and allow God to bring refreshing to your heart as He did mine.

> *If the goal is to be supernatural, you will end up in shipwreck. But if the goal is intimacy with Jesus, you will end up supernatural.*
> ~ *R. Loren Sandford*

This article was written by Jeremiah Johnson and used with permission (with minimal editing for readability and clarity).

About the Movie:
VOICE OF GOD

Do you want to experience the nearness of God every day? Do you want to be able to discern His voice with clarity? Do you want to participate with God in transforming the world around you so that His will is done on earth just like it is in Heaven?

VOICE OF GOD is a life-changing movie from the filmmakers who brought you PAID IN FULL (a movie that has activated countless people to minister healing in Jesus' name). In this most recent two-part film, Art Thomas invites you on a journey of learning to experience God's voice and participate with Him in His mission.

- o Learn from around 50 people some of the most practical and powerful advice about hearing God,
- o Watch what happens when people are led by the Holy Spirit (even into dangerous situations), and
- o Learn how you too can converse with God daily!

Experience a production that is more than a two-part film. Discover the joy and security of hearing God, knowing God, and partnering with Him to change the world!

Order your copy today at:
www.SupernaturalTruth.com

About the Movie:
PAID IN FULL

Imagine what would happen if every Christian was equipped to minister physical healing the way Jesus did. That's God's plan for the Church!

In Acts 5:12 and 16, we learn that the believers all met together in a part of the Temple called Solomon's Colonnade, and every sick and tormented person who came to them was healed. In the ministry of Jesus, everyone who touched His body was healed. (See Matthew 14:35-36; Mark 6:56; Luke 4:40; and Luke 6:18-19.) Now, WE are His Body! (See 1 Corinthians 12:27.)

PAID IN FULL is a film about God's continued desire to heal the sick, the diseased, the infirmed, the disabled, and the injured through ordinary people just like you. Meet more than 30 people who practice Christian healing ministry, and:

- o Witness instant miracles happening in public,
- o Hear testimonies of medically-documented healings, and
- o Learn how you too can minister healing in Jesus' name!

Experience a movie like none other. Discover more than what is happening throughout the world; JOIN IN!

Order your copy today at:
www.PaidInFullFilm.com